Diverticulitis Cookbook

A Comprehensive 3-Phase Diet Guide with 200 Proven & Delicious Diverticulitis Diet Recipes to Feel Great & Improve Gut Health. Easy to Find Ingredients & 21-Day Action Plan

Author: Sophie Robinson

Contents

What Exactly is Diverticulitis?

Diverticular disease, also referred to as diverticulitis, is an illness that causes tiny, inflamed sac-like pouches to form on your intestinal walls. These sacs protrude through the colon's outer walls creating pockets known as diverticula. This disease can be considered a silent killer as it is entirely possible for it to be present yet undetected if the symptoms are mild. The symptoms could be as mild as light diarrhea or even constipation which can be mistaken as normal. These symptoms would continue to worsen until it develops into your first flare-up. As the disease progresses, it goes through various stages. Each stage creates more diverticula (the small pouches mentioned earlier) causing some patients to suffer from thousands of small sacs that grow in size. On the flip side, many patients only have a single small sac (known as a diverticulum) generally with a diameter of less than a centimeter, though the possibility exists of the sac multiplying or growing over time.

The Latest Science on Diverticulitis

Over the past few years, numerous studies have been carried out on the causes, symptoms, and possible treatments for diverticulitis. In the past five years, more and more countries have issued guidelines on diverticulitis with differences regarding covered topics and recommendations including treatments. Presently, there is a lack of certainty on the impact of different drugs on patients who suffer from asymptomatic diverticulosis. A silver lining, however, is that throughout the years of research, limited indications have suggested that a progressive increase in dietary fiber aids in reducing the risk of developing diverticulitis.

Causes and Symptoms of Diverticulitis

Scientists have carried out intensive research over the years but have unfortunately not been able to hammer down a definite cause for diverticulitis. The one commonality among all their findings, however, was that a large number of the subjects who developed the disease happened to be people who lacked sufficient fiber in the way they chose to eat and live their lives. Despite the fact that no concrete evidence of a specific cause was found, many theories have surfaced throughout the years as to what the cause may be. One such theory that has grown in popularity believes that diverticulitis occurs as a result of pressure on the colon during constipation. It argues that straining when constipated causes the small diverticula to balloon from the intestinal wall and lodges between the muscle bundles from build up inside the colon. This theory, of course, has never been proven but it is the most logical theory to date. It goes further to pair the disease with age as the mass of the colon thickens as we get older. Though the reasoning behind the specific aspect is still unclear, it is argued to be comparable to the expanding weights required to help our colon dispose of feces.

A large number of patients suffering from diverticular disease experience unnecessary thickening of the solid mass of the colon that acts as the diverticular structure. The muscle in this area also contracts much stronger. It has also been argued that these muscle irregularities may very well contribute to the development of diverticular disease.

Closer examination of the edges of the diverticular structure in numerous studies has hinted at irritation and possible aggravation, which has also led some scientists to believe that this disturbance in the colon may not be a result of the disease but a determining factor of the arrangement of the diverticula.The ugly truth is that any of these possible theories could potentially be true. Without diving into the science itself, it is impossible to pinpoint which ones hit the nail on the head. What we can narrow down, however, is how the presence of diverticula affects the human body. With that in mind, let's explore a few of the main symptoms experienced when a person contracts diverticulitis.

Symptoms of Diverticulitis

Many diverticulitis patients do not experience daily symptoms outside of a flare-up. This, as you can imagine, makes diagnosis difficult outside of routine tests for general digestive issues. This isn't the reality for all patients; some patients experience warning signs or symptoms including:

Severe Constipation

Constipation can become so severe in diverticulitis patients that it prevents the passage of both gas and stool through the large intestine, and hence, a person is unable to pass the unwanted nitrogenous wastes out of the body.

Severe Pain in the Abdomen

Some may argue that abdominal pain is the most frequent symptom as over 95% of patients experience cramps in the left lower portion of the abdomen. These cramps can vary from person to person, but has been generally described as an achy, dull, or even sharp pain in some cases. At times, this pain may radiate to the lower back. The pain is sudden and severe in most cases, but it can also be mild in some cases.

Fever

Many patients experience a light fever in the early stages of diverticulitis and while it isn't a defining factor it does suggest the presence of an underlying infection. It is often associated with altered bowel habits, chills or both.

Diverticular Bleeding

Though bleeding isn't common, it does occur in some patients. On the off chance that you have bleeding, it can be serious. Fortunately, the bleeding in some cases may also stop on its own without requiring any form of treatment. Nonetheless, if you begin to experience any form of bleeding from your rectum, regardless of the amount, you should see a medical professional immediately. To discover the site of the bleeding and stop it, a specialist may perform a colonoscopy. Your specialist may likewise utilize an automated tomography (CT) check or an angiogram to discover the bleeding site. An angiogram is a unique sort of x-ray beam in which your specialist strings a dainty, adaptable tube through an extensive corridor, usually from your crotch to the bleeding region.

Urinary Symptoms

Another symptom that is not as widely linked to diverticulitis is urinary tract issues. These can vary from a burning sensation during urination, frequent urination, and other urinary-related issues due to the position of the bladder and colon in the body.

Nausea & Vomiting

Diverticulitis patients often suffer from indigestion-related symptoms such as nausea, vomiting and heartburn.

When controlled, diverticulitis oftentimes doesn't severely affect your life outside of a flare-up. On the flip side, however, when the symptoms are left uncontrolled until it's too late, several more serious complications can pop up as a result. Including, but not limited to intestinal perforation, fistula or abscess formation, peritonitis, bleeding and stricture (blockade).

These complications are often rare and mainly in patients who already have a compromised or weak immune system, for example, those with previous underlying autoimmune or chronic illnesses such as AIDs, cancer, heart disease, and diabetes to name a few. Or patients who have been taking steroids for a long period.

When Should I Seek Medical Assistance?

Go to an emergency care instantly in the likelihood that you have known diverticula or past episodes of diverticulitis and you encounter any of the accompanying symptoms:

- Steady fever along with stomach torment
- Serious stomach torment
- Steady obstruction with stomach swelling or bloating
- Serious torment or different symptoms you have experienced before during a diverticulitis session
- Serious vomiting

How to Improve Gut Flora

The human body is comprised of over 40 trillion bacteria that have multiple purposes, many of which reside in your intestines. The good bacteria as a collective are referred to as the gut microbiota or gut flora, and they play an extremely vital part in maintaining your overall health. The bad bacteria that form, on the other hand, contribute to many different diseases.

Due to this, it is vital that you take care of your gut to ensure that most of the bacteria residing in your body are good bacteria. As you may have already guessed, the food you consume plays a significant role in the type of bacteria that grow inside you.

Let's explore a few simple ways you can improve your gut flora:

- Maintaining Bacterial Balance

One of the symptoms that are very common in diverticulitis patients is intestinal bacterial overgrowth. That is too much development of harmful bacteria which leads to inflammation and damage to the entire system and makes all digestion less effective. Rifaximin is a drug that has been shown to affect this issue positively by returning the bacterial balance to a more normal level. Some simple foods will do this as well, including some specialty yogurts.

- Take Related Supplements

A person suffering from diverticulitis may be able to find some significant relief by taking probiotic supplements. In combination with other treatments, the probiotic nutrients can give a person a whole new lease on life. Some great food choices already include probiotics in them for example eating foods containing kefir, kimchi or kombucha will naturally help reduce the effects of diverticulitis.

Adding a supplement like Prescript Assist or VSL#3 is not a bad idea—no matter how your current health is— because it will improve your digestion and allow you to feel healthier each day.

- Probiotics

It is important to make sure probiotics are present in your diet. Probiotics will add healthy bacteria to the digestive system and make the colon work smoother and more efficiently which will allow for less development of diverticular disease. Probiotics enhance the ability of the body to take the nutrients from food, break down lactose and even help improve the immune system of the body. Low-fat yogurt or kefir is a great source of probiotics for people to consume to help avoid diverticular disease.

Prebiotics are another option when it comes to correcting the level of good/bad bacteria in the digestive system. These are substances that are known to develop and nurture the growth and development of the positive forms of bacteria that will keep you healthy and manage your wellbeing.

This is exactly what a person is looking for when they need to restore a healthy bacterial balance. One great prebiotic is fructose-oligosaccharide powder but consult a doctor to learn more about prebiotics that can help solve a poor bacterial balance and help to stop diverticulitis before it begins.

Stay away from foods high in fat. It is no secret that foods that are high in fat tend to slow down the digestion process and can lead to episodes of constipation. This is not healthy for the colon because it causes undue stress on the muscles and can cause long-term damage to them. It is also much easier to maintain a healthy weight if foods that are high in fat are avoided.

- Eat Regularly

It is important to develop a normal eating schedule each day. It is believed that eating all of your snacks and meals at the same time each day will allow your digestive system and colon to work more regularly and will keep your colon in great shape and avoid the development of diverticular disease. Set a goal to have your three main meals at about the same time each day along with any snacks. Most people are creatures of habit, and this can become easy to do.

- Lean Meats

If you are going to consume meats, ensure they are lean meats. Meats that have an excess of fatty tissue in them are not healthy for digestion and they can introduce too much of the unhealthy kinds of bacteria into the colon—a perceived cause of diverticulitis. Some smart meats to eat are skinless poultry, pork loin and select lean cuts of steak.

- Gain an Understanding of Fiber and How It Affects Your Gut

Doctors that specialized in digestive tract illnesses have looked at what most people eat as a daily part of their diet and found that it is lacking in many of the essential nutrients that people should be eating for excellent digestive health. One of these ingredients is a diet that is much higher in fiber than was previously prescribed. One of the major contributors to the development of diverticulitis is that a person has difficulty in passing waste out of the colon through the rectum.

A diet high in fiber will make this much easier and alleviate much of the problem. After the muscles in a person's colon spend years of straining to perform their function due to a diet that is low in fiber there is a development of this issue. Particularly in the United States, this is prevalent. Doctors start to realize that the colon is becoming a bit stretched which makes it even more difficult to pass excrement from the body and the stool needs to be even bulkier to be moved out without difficulty.

A study was carried out by the Journal of Nutrition that involved nearly 45,000 health professionals participating in a long-term study. They learned that when a person ate a diet that was high in fiber, they lowered the risk of contracting diverticular disease by somewhere in the range of 40%.
A high-fiber diet presents a lot of other benefits as well. It fills your stomach easily and suppresses your appetite which can be a major aid in losing weight. Losing weight can help to fight the development of diverticular disease indirectly. Diverticular disease is much more likely to put a woman in the hospital if she is overweight or inactive. This is according to a study that was published in the American Journal of Gastroenterology.

The current recommendation is that 25 grams of fiber should be consumed by women each and every day. While men should eat even more fiber, they are advised to try to consume about 38 grams of fiber in their daily diet. Even with these warnings, the average American eats about 15 grams of fiber—a woefully low portion. One of the best ways to increase your lack of fiber is to include foods that are high in fiber at every meal and also in snacks throughout the day. Great sources of fiber for your diet include whole grains, oatmeal, whole wheat bread, and barley. There are also some other great foods that you can dig into like lentils, fruits, vegetables and beans to give your diet a boost. One of the best snacking foods for a higher fiber intake into your diet is to eat plenty of dried fruits which are a terrific source of fiber.

This type of eating plan is referred to as a whole foods diet because it includes a lot of foods that are not processed and treated with chemicals like white rice and white bread. Both of these are going to aid in causing diverticulitis rather than preventing it. Eliminating the food that is bad for you is just as important as adding food that is good for the body.

There are two types of fiber to consider—soluble and insoluble. They are both an important part of a healthy diet but for different reasons. The insoluble fiber found in vegetable peels of fruit and seeds will add bulk to the stool in the colon and make it easier to pass reducing the burdening strain on the muscle. Soluble fiber is the other type that a body needs, and it comes from foods like oatmeal, barley, and many fresh fruits like apples. This adds to the moisture located in the stool and makes it easier to pass through the colon and reduces the strain.

The recommended intake of fiber is generally:
- Women aged 19 to 50 = 25 grams per day
- Women aged 50+ = 21 grams per day
- Men aged 19 to 50 = 38 grams per day
- Men aged 50+ = 30 grams per day

Please contact your doctor to confirm that these values are okay for your specific scenario.

- Drink More Fluids

Many overlook the importance of staying hydrated, but this tip may be the most important in maintaining gut health. Drinking more fluids can help a high-fiber diet move even easier through the digestive system with fewer chances of obstructions developing. A normal fluid intake is all that is needed. There doesn't seem to be much of a benefit for drinking excessive liquids during the day. Look to drink as many non-calorie beverages as you can with your diet each day which means no limits to water or tea.

The recommended water intake is generally:
- Men aged 19+ = 12 cups (about 3 liters) per day
- Women aged 19+ = 9 cups (about 2 liters) per day

Please contact your doctor to confirm that these values are okay for your specific scenario.

Approved Diverticulitis Foods

It is important to remember that having diverticulitis does not mean that a person is going to have any observable and visible symptoms. Many people live blissfully unaware of their condition until they have an attack and then that painful uncomfortable condition will need to be treated by a doctor. One of the simple treatments is with antibiotics but there are more serious cases that need to be handled with surgery.

Again, we know that if you are suffering from diverticulitis, a liquid diet may be prescribed by your doctor as a part of your treatment. This will give the colon a chance to heal and recover without having to perform the task it was designed for.

This type of liquid diet should include water, fruit juices, broth, ice pops and tea. Very slowly the patient can start easing back into eating solid foods. However, at this point, fiber intake should not be neglected, and the patient should start eating high-fiber foods. Because of the medical condition, the colon might have difficulty at first passing high-fiber foods very well so your doctor will most likely prescribe foods that are lower in fiber, to begin with.

These include eggs, fish, poultry and all dairy products as well. Remember the more fiber that is present in the diet the more bulk there will be in the stool and that will reduce the pressure on the colon to perform its job.

Studies have been performed that demonstrate clearly that fiber-rich foods can help control the symptoms that diverticulitis brings about. Again, it is of great importance that you try to eat at least 25–35 grams of fiber each and every day.

There are three main phases of the diverticulitis diet: eating during an active flare-up, eating while recovering from a flare-up, and preventing a flare-up in the future. As with any other diet, you will need to listen to your body throughout each stage and adjust the diet slowly as you add new foods while closely monitoring your symptoms.

Phase 1: Clear Fluids (During a Flare-Up)
While going through an active flare-up, your symptoms can become extreme. Due to this, it's smart for you to give your bowel a period of rest. As you can imagine, the best way to do this is by sticking to a clear fluid diet. This will aid in your recovery as your body may outright reject solid foods.

It is vital to note that the clear fluid stage of the diet is NOT intended to be a long-term diet. In fact, the general expectation is that you remain in this stage for no more than a couple of days.

Please Note:
Restricting yourself to a clear fluid diet for an excessive amount of time may cause you to feel light-headed, weak, hungry, and fatigued. You can also experience muscle wasting, excessive weight loss, and depletion of vitamins and minerals.

This occurs due to the fact that it's incredibly difficult to meet the body's daily caloric requirements for fat, protein, and carbohydrates during a clear fluid diet. The average person will need to provide their body with at least 200 grams of carbohydrates to have enough energy to go through the day. If you struggle with low blood sugar, diabetes, or other blood sugar challenges, you may want to monitor your blood sugar levels during this stage.

As the name implies, this phase is composed of clear liquids. These include green tea, fresh fruit juice, clear broth, and gelatin dessert. The clear liquid diet provides the body with salt, liquids, and enough nutrients to function temporarily, **generally for a few days,** until you can eat normal food again.

Phase 2: Low-Residue/Low-Fiber Diet (Immediately after a Controlled Flare-Up)

A low-residue (or low-fiber) diet acts as the reintroduction phase, after your flare-up symptoms have mostly passed but before your body is ready for high-fiber or high residue foods.

Phase 3: High-Fiber Meals (Daily Life/ Preventing Future Flare-Ups)

This final stage in the diverticulitis diet is the high-fiber diet. This stage is used to maintain a balanced diet while preventing a future flare-up. It is basically your general day-to-day eating routine, and generally takes up the majority of your diverticulitis eating plan.

It is important to note, however, that you do not want to jump directly from a significantly low-fiber diet (such as a clear fluid diet) to a high-fiber diet, as this will do more harm to your colon than good. It is always best to ease into any stage of the plan that requires an increase in your fiber intake. Aim to increase your fiber intake by 2 to 4 grams per week until you reach the recommended amount for your age and biology. Bear in mind that as you increase your fiber, you also need to increase your water intake to help move the fiber through your intestinal tract.

Essential Shopping List

Fruits
- ❖ Apple Sauce
- ❖ Apples
- ❖ Apricots
- ❖ Bananas
- ❖ Dates
- ❖ Mangoes
- ❖ Oranges
- ❖ Peaches
- ❖ Prunes

Juices
- ❖ Apple Juice
- ❖ Lemon Juice
- ❖ Lime Juice
- ❖ Orange Juice
- ❖ Cranberry Juice

Vegetables
- ❖ Alfalfa Sprouts
- ❖ Artichoke Hearts
- ❖ Asparagus
- ❖ Avocados
- ❖ Black Olives
- ❖ Broccoli
- ❖ Butternut Squash
- ❖ Cabbage
- ❖ Carrots
- ❖ Cauliflower
- ❖ Celery
- ❖ Eggplants
- ❖ Garlic
- ❖ Green Bell Peppers (seedless)
- ❖ Green Olives
- ❖ Green Onions

- ❖ Leeks
- ❖ Mushrooms
- ❖ Lettuce
- ❖ Olives
- ❖ Onions
- ❖ Peas (frozen, cooked)
- ❖ Pimento
- ❖ Red Bell Peppers (seedless)
- ❖ Russet Potatoes
- ❖ Shallots
- ❖ Spinach
- ❖ Sugar Snap Peas
- ❖ Summer Squash
- ❖ Yellow Peppers (seedless)
- ❖ Tomatoes (seedless)
- ❖ Water Chestnuts
- ❖ Zucchini
- ❖ Sweet Yams

Beans & Peas
- ❖ Black Beans
- ❖ Butter Beans
- ❖ Cannellini Beans
- ❖ Garbanzo Beans
- ❖ Canned Kidney Beans
- ❖ Lentils
- ❖ Canned Lima Beans
- ❖ Canned Navy Beans
- ❖ Canned Red Beans

Grains, Breads & Other Starches

- ❖ All-Bran Cereal
- ❖ Barley
- ❖ Brown Rice
- ❖ Fiber One Cereal
- ❖ Long Grain Rice
- ❖ Oat Bran
- ❖ Rolled Oats
- ❖ Whole Wheat Tortellini
- ❖ Whole Wheat Flour
- ❖ Whole Wheat Pasta
- ❖ Whole Wheat Pita
- ❖ Whole Wheat Tortillas
- ❖ Whole Wheat Bread

Meats

- ❖ Crab Meat (cooked)
- ❖ Ground Chicken (lean)
- ❖ Ground Turkey (lean)
- ❖ Lean Ham
- ❖ Shrimp (large, peeled)
- ❖ Canned Tuna Fish (in water)
- ❖ Turkey Breast
- ❖ Chicken Breast

Dairy

- ❖ Cheddar Cheese (low fat)
- ❖ Cottage Cheese (low fat)
- ❖ Cream Cheese (low fat)
- ❖ Feta Cheese
- ❖ Monterrey Jack Cheese (low fat)
- ❖ Parmesan Cheese
- ❖ Eggs
- ❖ Half and Half Cream
- ❖ Milk (low fat)

- ❖ Yogurt (low fat)

Spices, Herbs & Oils

- ❖ Baking Powder
- ❖ Basil (fresh or dried)
- ❖ Canola Oil
- ❖ Cilantro (fresh)
- ❖ Cinnamon Powder
- ❖ Cumin
- ❖ Curry Powder
- ❖ Dill, (fresh or dried)
- ❖ Italian Seasoning
- ❖ Nutmeg
- ❖ Olive Oil
- ❖ Oregano (fresh and dried)
- ❖ Parsley, Italian (fresh)
- ❖ Sage (fresh)
- ❖ Tarragon (fresh)
- ❖ Thyme (fresh and dried)
- ❖ Vanilla

Condiments

- Vegetable Stock
- Chicken Stock
- Coconut Milk
- Dijon Mustard
- Honey
- Light Ranch Dressing
- Maple Syrup
- Mayonnaise (low fat)
- Red Wine Vinegar
- Rice Vinegar
- Soy Sauce
- Sweet Pickle Relish
- Tarragon Vinegar
- Tomato Paste
- Tomato Sauce
- Tomato Puree
- Canned Tomato (diced, seedless)

List of Foods to Avoid

Patients with diverticulitis are often urged to exercise caution when consuming seeds or anything with seeds (i.e., tomatoes, melons, berries, etc.). Small food particles such as seeds are theorized to potentially be able to get logged in the diverticulum and cause inflammation. Although there hasn't been any scientific evidence to date that would confirm this belief, I will be including seeds and nuts in our *Foods to Avoid List* and omit them from my recipes. Be sure to consult your doctor to check whether you would be permitted to include them in your diet.

There are several reasons why certain foods should be avoided during the acute (symptomatic) phase of diverticulitis. Some of these reasons include:

- Increase the bulk of the stool: some of these foods are high in fiber and, therefore, contribute to the consistency and bulk of the stool. In many cases, as a person already suffers from severe constipation, increased intake of such foods will only make it harder to defecate and will eventually result in more abdominal discomfort.
- Some of these foods can get caught in the pouches called diverticula.
- Take a longer time for digestion: some of these foods take a longer time to digest. As the digestive system is already sore (inflamed), and under abnormally high pressure during diverticulitis, more of such foods will only create more complications, and as a result, the stomach and intestines would not get the much-needed "rest" during diverticulitis.
- Produce flatulence and bloating: intestinal gas and bloating are common side effects of a high-fiber diet. The presence of such symptoms will increase the risk of more complications during a diverticulitis attack.

Vegetables with Small Particles or Seeds

- Cucumber (only English is acceptable)
- Green Peppers (Acceptable if seeds are removed)
- Tomato (Acceptable if seeds are removed)
- Chili Peppers
- Corn

Seeds & Nuts
- Avoid all types

Sweets with Small Particles or Seeds
- Nutty Candy
- Fruit Jam with Seeds
- Nutty Desserts
- Raisins with Seeds

Fruits with Small Particles or Seeds
- Blackberries
- Blueberries
- Coconut (dried)
- Whole Cranberries (cranberry relish)
- Figs
- Grapes (with seeds)
- Kiwi
- Pomegranates
- Raspberries
- Strawberries
- Watermelon (acceptable if seedless)

Starches (Refined)
- Bread or rolls with nuts/seeds
- Popcorn
- Wild Rice

How to Prevent and Deal with Attacks

Patients may have various signs of diverticular disease or diverticulitis and it might be hard to differentiate the two. Milder signs of torment might be dealt with at home with bed rest, prescriptions for torment and fit, and a distinct fluid diet. Patients ought to take their temperature as often as possible and push on their lower left guts where most diverticula are found.

At the principal indication of fever or expanding delicacy—indications of aggravation—a specialist ought to be consulted immediately for a conceivable visit to his office and/or the start of anti-infection agents; there is nothing as beneficial as a physical examination by a specialist to settle on choices about further treatment or hospitalization.

How to Deal with Mild to Medium Symptoms

Most patients with diverticulosis have negligible or no symptoms and don't require any particular treatment. A typical fiber diet is appropriate to counteract blockage and maybe prevent the arrangement of more diverticula. Patients with mild symptoms of stomach pain because of strong fit in the range of the Diverticular may profit by hostile to uncontrollable medications, for example:

- Hyoscyamine (Levsin)
- Phenobarbital (Donnatal)
- Chlordiazepoxide (Librax)
- Dicyclomine (Bentyl)
- Scopolamine
- Atropine

When diverticulitis occurs, anti-toxins are usually required. Oral anti-infection agents are adequate when symptoms are mild.

A few types of generally recommended antimicrobials include:

- Flagyl (Metronidazole)
- Cipro (Ciprofloxacin)
- Keflex (Cephalexin)
- Vibramycin (Doxycycline)

What are different medications for diverticulitis?

Fluid or low-fiber foods are suggested during intense attacks of diverticulitis. The purpose is to decrease the amount of material that goes through the colon, which in any event hypothetically, may irritate the diverticulitis. In extreme diverticulitis, where patients suffer from intense pain and high fever, the patients are often hospitalized to be treated with intravenous anti-infection agents. Surgery is required for patients with steady entrails obstacle, bleeding, or sore not reacting to antibiotics.

How to Deal with Severe Symptoms

Diverticulitis that does not react to restorative treatment requires surgical mediation. Surgery normally includes drainage of any collections of discharge and resection (surgical evacuation) of the portion of the colon containing the diverticula, as a rule, the sigmoid colon. Surgical expulsion of the bleeding diverticulum likewise is important for those with determined bleeding. In patients requiring surgery to stop industrious bleeding, it is important to determine precisely where the bleeding is originating from with the end goal to direct the specialist.

Now and then, diverticula can disintegrate into the nearby urinary bladder, creating serious intermittent pee contamination and entry of gas amid pee. This circumstance additionally requires surgery.

Now and then, surgery might be proposed for patients with regular, repetitive attacks of diverticulitis prompting different courses of anti-toxins, hospitalizations, and days lost from work. During surgery, the objective is to remove all of the colon containing diverticula to prevent future occurrences of diverticulitis.

21-Day Action Plan for Diverticulitis

Having a diverticulitis flare-up can be a stressful and painful experience. Many times, during your actual flare-up a clear liquid diet (discussed in more detail below) will help ease your symptoms. Afterwards however, understanding when and how to reintroduce fiber can be tricky as it can cause the flare-up to worsen if not done correctly,

Let's explore a 21-day action plan to assist you in reintroducing fiber into your diet safely. **Please be sure to consult your doctor on your specific condition before embarking on this action or meal plan.**

Phase 1 (Days 1–7 of a Flare-Up – Clear Liquid Diet

While experiencing a diverticulitis flare-up, or at the first sign of symptoms, it is imperative that you give your digestive tract a break to cleanse and heal itself. During the first few days to a week of your flare-up or symptoms, it is recommended that you consume a clear liquid diet of clear soups, broths, teas and even ice pops. An example of a recipe you can enjoy during this phase is featured below and you can find many other recipes to mix and match in the recipe section of this cookbook.

Yields: 6 cups   Prep: 10 mins.   Cook: 3-1/4 hours

Nutrition per Serving:

245 calories, 14 g fat, 8 g carbs, 2 g fiber, 21g protein

Ingredients:

- chicken neck (2 lbs.)
- celery ribs with leaves (2, cut into chunks)
- carrots (2 medium, cut into chunks)
- onions (2 medium, quartered)
- bay leaves (2)
- rosemary (1/2 teaspoon dried, crushed)
- thyme (1/2 teaspoon dried)
- peppercorns (8 to 10 whole corns)
- cold water (2 quarts)

Directions:

1. Transfer the bones and vegetables to your stockpot. Top with enough water to cover then allow to slowly come to a boil on high heat.
2. Switch to low heat and simmer for at least 2 hours and up to 12 hours. (The longer it cooks, the more flavor you will get.)
3. Carefully pour the mixture through a fine mesh strainer into a large bowl. Taste and season with salt.
4. Serve hot.

Bone stock with cooked vegetables and a little bit of meat provides the key supplements your body needs, including calcium, magnesium, phosphorus, silicon, sulfur—and that's just the beginning, in an effortlessly processed way.

You may add vegetables to your bone stock including carrots, celery and garlic, or for variety you may include an egg poached in the stock. Furthermore, sip on warm ginger tea a few times every day to reduce aggravation and help in assimilation. Ginger is a healing food that helps your resistance and digestive systems.

For beef, the collagen in the bones separates into gelatin in around 48 hours, and for chicken, it takes around 24 hours. You can make soup in less time, yet to get the most out of the bones, I suggest making it in a stewing pot for more like 48 hours.

Gelatin has stunning curative properties and even helps people with food sensitivities and hypersensitivities endure these foods all the more effortlessly. It likewise advances probiotic parity, while separating proteins making them less demanding to process. The reality about probiotic and digestive issues is that they make a solid situation in your paunch. During this first period of the diverticulitis diet, devour just clear bone juices, clear crisp squeezes no ash), and calming ginger tea.

Phase 2 (Days 7–14 after a Flare-Up) – Low-Residue/Fiber Diet

About 7 days after a treated diverticulitis flare-up, you can proceed to phase two of the diverticulitis diet and SLOWLY reintroduce fiber into your diet. We refer to this phase as the low-residue diet as during this week you will be able to enjoy low-fiber meals along with clear fluids if you so desire.

Juicing new natural foods grown from the ground can be supportive to supplements. Vegetables and fruits like watercress, lettuce, apples, grapes, beets and carrots can be used to make juices that can be useful during this stage. Maintain a strategic distance from foods with extreme skins and little seeds as they can aggregate in the diverticular sacs.

One such example recipe of this phase is:

Slow Cooker Salsa Turkey

Yields: 8   Prep: 5 mins.   Cook: 8 hrs.

Nutrition per Serving:

178 calories, 4 g fat, 7 g carbs, 2 g fiber, 27 g protein

Ingredients:

- turkey breasts (2 pounds, boneless and skinless)
- salsa (1 cup)
- tomatoes (1 cup, petite, diced, canned, choose low sodium)
- taco seasoning (2 tablespoons)
- celery (1/2 cup, diced fine)
- carrots (1/2 cup, shredded)
- sour cream (3 tablespoons, reduced fat)

Directions:

1. Add your turkey to your slow cooker. Season your turkey with taco seasoning then top with your salsa and vegetables.
2. Add in a ½ cup of water. Set to cook on low for 7 hours (internal temperature should be 165°F when done).
3. Shred the turkey with 2 forks, add in sour cream and stir. Enjoy.

Phase 3 (Days 15–21 Daily Life Outside of Flare-Ups) – **_High-Fiber Diet_**

At the point when your body has adjusted to the foods in the low-residue stage, begin to include fiber-rich foods including crude products from the soil, and grungy grains, for example, quinoa, dark rice, matured grains, or sprouted lentils. It is essential to avoid whole nuts and seeds, as they can without much of a stretch get caught in the diverticula, causing additional harm.

While seeds, nuts and popcorn are not the reason for diverticulitis, during this phase in healing, it is best to maintain a strategic distance from them. Once your diverticulitis symptoms have ebbed, you can come back to getting a charge out of these foods, and others, with some restraint.

Listen to your body; if anytime you begin to experience diverticulitis symptoms once more, return to the previous stage. It might take a couple of months to totally heal your digestive tract.

An example recipe in this stage is:

Pear Turkey Pita

Yields: 4   Prep: 15 mins.   Cook: 0 mins.
Nutrition per Serving:
221 calories, 3 g fat, 21 g carbs, 2 g fiber, 25 g protein

Ingredients:
- turkey (2 cups, cooked, cubed)
- pears (2, medium, unpeeled, chopped)
- celery (1 stalk, chopped)
- yogurt (1/3 cup, plain, low-fat or non-fat)
- mayonnaise (1/4 cup, non-fat)
- pita breads (4, round, whole wheat)
- lettuce leaves (4, romaine)

Directions:
1. In a bowl, combine the turkey, celery, and pears. Add mayonnaise and yogurt then combine. Create a pocket by slicing a pita.
2. Put the lettuce leaf inside the pita and fill the pocket with 1 cup of mixture in each pita bread.
3. Serve with mixed fruits. Do not include berries).

As indicated by analysts at the University of Oxford, fiber reduces the danger of diverticular disease. The study concentrated on fiber from natural products, vegetables, oats, and potatoes. So, over the initial few days of stage four, introduce high-fiber foods bit by bit, including only one new nourishment each 3–4 days. As your body adjusts you can start consuming around 25–35 grams of fiber every day, to combat potential flare-ups while your body heals your digestive tract. Include a few potatoes, sweet potatoes, root vegetables, then gradually try some non-prepared grains/beans, for example, oats or lentils. One important qualification is the difference between soluble fiber and insoluble fiber. Dissolvable fiber really holds water and transforms into a gel during the digestive process. The gel moderates the processing, considering more prominent assimilation of key supplements. Insoluble fiber, then again, adds mass to stools, permitting foods to all the more rapidly leave your system.Foods high in dissolvable fiber include oat grain, nuts, seeds, beans, lentils grain, and peas. Insoluble fiber is found in foods including whole grains, wheat grain, and vegetables. Scientists at the Department of Nutrition at Harvard Medical School found that it is the insoluble fiber that decreases the danger of developing diverticular disease. Be that as it may, don't let this influence you from eating an adjusted diet. You don't need to avoid dissolvable fiber, nor if you. Keeping up a sound parity of protein, fiber, and crisp leafy foods, is key for keeping diverticulitis from erupting.

Be Sure to Incorporate Supplements That Offer:

Aloe
Aloe in juice form helps with absorption, standardizes pH levels, regularizes bowel handling, and energizes the digestive microorganisms. It is important to maintain a strategic distance from aloe Vera juice with "aloe latex," as it can cause severe stomach cramping and diarrhea. Twelve to 16 ounces of aloe juice daily is prescribed; any more than that can aggravate your system.

Slippery Elm

Local Americans have utilized dangerous elm for quite a long time both remotely, and inside to soothe digestive issues and relieve coughs and sore throats. Today, it is prescribed to relieve the symptoms of GERD, Crohn's disease, IBS, and digestive miracle. Begin by taking 500 milligrams, 3 times daily, throughout the diverticulitis diet. Make sure to take it with a full glass of water, or other clear fluid.

Licorice Root

Licorice Root is great for reducing acid levels in your stomach. It can also aid in relieving acid reflux and acting as a mild laxative to clear your colon of waste. This root expands bile, supporting absorption, while bringing down cholesterol levels. Take 100 milligrams every day while encountering diverticulitis symptoms.

Digestive Enzymes

In addition to healing your colon from diverticulitis, the general objective of the diverticulitis diet, supplements, and way of life changes, is to help your digestive tract to work properly.
Digestive enzymes separate foods, making it conceivable to assimilate supplements. People with assimilation issues can take digestive supplements that contain crucial catalysts to encourage absorption.

Probiotics

Live probiotics ought to be added to the diet to invalidate food sensitivities, and relieve digestive upset including blockage, gas, and bloating. Probiotics are sound microscopic organisms that generally line your digestive tract to fight off disease. On the off chance that you have diverticulitis, you require an influx of these microorganisms to help with the healing of your colon, while preventing disease recurrence.

Sample 21-Day Diverticulitis Meal Plan For

Incorporating All Three Stages of the Diet

Let's explore a sample 21-day meal plan using the recipes featured in this book for incorporating everyday meals into the three phases of the diverticulitis diet to successfully recover from and prevent future flare-ups.

There are 200 delicious recipes in the sections that follow so please feel free to mix and match recipes to suit your personal taste and circumstances.

Remember this meal plan is meant for informational purposes only. Everybody is different and as such their flare-ups and speed of recovery may differ. So be sure to speak to a medical professional to make sure this meal plan would be best for you.

Day	Breakfast/Brunch	Lunch/Dinner	Snack	Supper/Dessert
Day 1 (During the Flare)	Cinnamon Orange Tea	Oxtail Bone Broth	Pineapple Ice Cubes	Frozen Strawberry – Peach Pop
Day 2 (During the Flare)	Kiwi Cinnamon Tea	Homey Clear Chicken Broth	Autumn Energizer Juice	Honey Lemonade Popsicle

Day 3 (During the Flare)	Cranberry Green Tea	Fish Broth	Strawberry Gummies	Basil Watermelon Popsicle
Day 4 (During the Flare)	Blueberry Earl Grey Tea	Clear Pumpkin Broth	Fruity Jell-O Stars	Grapefruit Lemonade Popsicle
Day 5 (During the Flare)	Grape Mint Tea	Mushroom, Cauliflower & Cabbage Broth	Celery Apple Juice	Ginger Beer Gelatin Dessert
Day 6 (During the Flare)	Vanilla Plum Tea	Pork Stock	Pineapple Ginger Ice Cubes	Homemade Orange Gelatin
Day 7 (During the Flare)	Pineapple Old Spice Tea	Asian Inspired Wonton Broth	Elderberry Gummies	Raspberry Lemonade Popsicles

Day 8 (After the Flare)	Pear Pancakes	Pea Tuna Salad	Frozen Strawberry – Peach Pop	Grilled Lemon Rosemary Chicken
Day 9 (After the Flare)	Spiced Oatmeal	Haddock Noodle Soup	Honey Lemonade Popsicle	Roasted Salmon
Day 10 (After the Flare)	Zucchini Omelet	Saltfish Salad	Basil Watermelon Popsicle	Slow Cooker Salsa Turkey
Day 11 (After the Flare)	Strawberry Cashew Chia Pudding	Baked Sweet Potatoes	Grapefruit Lemonade Popsicle	Banana Cocoa Cream
Day 12 (After the Flare)	Breakfast Cereal	Mediterranean Salmon & Potato salad	Ginger Beer Gelatin Dessert	Oatmeal Cookie Smoothie
Day 13 (After the Flare)	Sweet Potato Hash with Sausage & Spinach	Celery Soup	Homemade Orange Gelatin	Spaghetti Squash in Tomato Sauce

Day 14 (After the Flare)	Apple Oatmeal	Dump Pot Chicken & Rice	Raspberry Lemonade Popsicles	Orange Curd
Day 15 (High Fiber/ Balanced Diet)	Veggie Scramble	Pork & Penne Pasta	Pineapple Ice Cubes	Mango Kale Smoothie
Day 16 (High Fiber/ Balanced Diet)	Overnight Oats	Vegetarian Rice Casserole	Autumn Energizer Juice	Sweet Potato Cream Pie
Day 17 (High Fiber/ Balanced Diet)	Pear Turkey Pita	Chicken Lettuce Wraps	Strawberry Gummies	Quinoa Risotto
Day 18 (High Fiber/ Balanced Diet)	Couscous with Dates	Rice Bowl with Shrimp & Peas	Fruity Jell-O Stars	Easy Turkey Chili

Day 19 (High Fiber/ Balanced Diet)	Black Bean Pita Pockets	Green Goodness Salad	Celery Apple Juice	Mushroom & Bean Stew
Day 20 (High Fiber/ Balanced Diet)	Spinach & Ham Pizza	Grilled Fish Tacos	Pineapple Ginger Ice Cubes	Asian Chicken Salad
Day 21 (High Fiber/ Balanced Diet)	Pork Fajitas	String Bean Potato Salad	Elderberry Gummies	Turkey Florentine

Now that we have explored the general background of diverticulitis, let's dive into 200 amazingly delicious recipes to get you on your way.

PHASE 1 RECIPES: Clear Fluids

Clear Broths & Stocks

Homey Clear Chicken Broth

Yields: 6 cups   Prep: 10 mins.   Cook: 3-1/4 hours

Nutrition per Serving:
245 calories, 14g fat, 8g carbs, 2g fiber, 21g protein

Ingredients:

- Chicken neck (2 lbs)
- celery ribs with leaves (2, cut into chunks)
- carrots (2 medium, cut into chunks)
- onions (2 medium, quartered)
- bay leaves (2)
- rosemary (1/2 teaspoon dried, crushed)
- thyme (1/2 teaspoon dried)
- peppercorns (8 to 10 whole)
- cold water (2 quarts)

Directions:

1. Transfer the bones and vegetables to your stockpot. Top with enough water to cover then allow to slowly come to a boil on high heat.
2. Switch to low heat and simmer for at least 2 hours and up to 12 hours. (The longer it cooks, the more flavor you will get.)
3. Carefully pour the mixture through a fine mesh strainer into a large bowl. Taste and season with salt.
4. Serve hot.

Oxtail Bone Broth

Yields: 8 cups   Prep: 15 mins.   Cook: 12 hours

Nutrition per Serving:

576 calories, 48 g fat, 8 g carbs, 0 g fiber, 24 g protein

Ingredients:

- Oxtail (2 Pounds)
- Onion (1, chopped in quarters)
- celery stalks (2, chopped in half)
- carrots (2, chopped in half)
- garlic cloves (3, whole)
- bay leaves (2)
- apple cider vinegar (2 Tablespoons)
- salt (1 Tablespoon)
- peppercorns (1/2 Tablespoon)
- filtered water (enough to cover bones)

Directions:

1. Transfer the bones and vegetables to your stockpot. Top with enough water to cover then allow to slowly come to a boil on high heat.
2. Switch to low heat and simmer for at least 2 hours and up to 12 hours. (The longer it cooks, the more flavor you will get.)
3. Carefully pour the mixture through a fine mesh strainer into a large bowl. Taste and season with salt.
4. Serve hot.

Asian Inspired Wonton Broth

Yields: 1-gallon   Prep: 5 mins.   Cook: 1 hour 35 mins.

Nutrition per Serving:
181 calories, 7 g fat, 14 g carbs, 1 g fiber, 14g protein

Ingredients:

- chicken thigh (1, skin on)
- carrot (1, coarsely chopped)
- celery (1 stalk, coarsely chopped)
- onion (1 small, quartered)
- ginger (3 dime-sized pieces)
- Kosher salt (2 tablespoons)
- Turmeric (1/4 teaspoon)
- MSG, (1/8 teaspoon, don't leave it out)
- Peppercorns (5 white, black can be substituted)
- Water (1 gallon)

Directions:

1. Transfer all your ingredients to your stockpot. Top with enough water to cover then allow to slowly come to a boil on high heat.
2. Switch to low heat and simmer for at least 1 hours and 30 minutes.
3. Carefully pour the mixture through a fine mesh strainer into a large bowl. Taste and season with salt.
4. Serve hot.

Mushroom, Cauliflower & Cabbage Broth

Serves: 3   Prep: 10 mins.   Cook: 50 mins.
Nutrition per Serving:
141 calories, 5g fat, 22g carbs, 7 g fiber, 5 g protein

Ingredients:

- ❖ yellow onion (1 large)
- ❖ celery stalks (1 cup, chopped)
- ❖ carrots (2 diced or cubed)
- ❖ French beans (10)
- ❖ cabbage (½ diced)
- ❖ celery leaves (1 to 2 stalks)

- ❖ mushrooms sliced (1½ cup)
- ❖ cauliflower (8 florets)
- ❖ garlic (1 tsp, chopped)
- ❖ ginger (1 tsp, chopped)
- ❖ oil (1 tbsp)
- ❖ scallions (1 stalk)
- ❖ pepper (½ tsp crushed)

Directions:

1. Transfer all your ingredients to your stockpot. Top with enough water to cover then allow to slowly come to a boil on high heat.
2. Switch to low heat and simmer for 50 minutes.
3. Carefully pour the mixture through a fine mesh strainer into a large bowl. Mash the veggies well to extract all their juices.
4. Taste and season with salt. Enjoy.

Indian Inspired Vegetable stock

Yields: 3 cups   Prep: 15 mins.   Cook: 11 mins.

Nutrition per Serving:

103 calories, 0.2mg fat, 23.3 g carbs, 3.1 g fiber, 2.2 g protein

Ingredients:

- Onions (3/4 cup, roughly chopped)
- Carrot (3/4 cup, roughly chopped)
- Tomatoes (3/4 cup, roughly chopped)
- Potatoes (3/4 cup, roughly chopped)
- Turmeric (1 tsp.)
- salt to taste

Directions:

1. Transfer your ingredients to your stockpot. Top with enough water to cover then allow to slowly come to a boil on high heat.
2. Switch to low heat and simmer for 11 minutes.
3. Carefully pour the mixture through a fine mesh strainer into a large bowl. Taste and season with salt.
4. Serve hot. Enjoy!

Beef Bone Broth

Yields: 8 cups   Prep: 15 mins.   Cook: 12 hours

Nutrition per Serving:

69 calories, 4 g fat, 1 g carbs, 0.1 g fiber, 6 g protein

Ingredients:

- beef bones (2 Pounds)
- onion (1, chopped in quarters)
- celery stalks (2, chopped in half)
- carrots (2, chopped in half)
- garlic cloves (3, whole)
- bay leaves (2)
- apple cider vinegar (2 Tablespoons)
- salt (1 Tablespoon)
- peppercorns (1/2 Tablespoon)
- filtered water (enough to cover bones)

Directions:

1. Transfer the bones and vegetables to your stockpot. Top with enough water to cover then allow to slowly come to a boil on high heat.
2. Switch to low heat and simmer for at least 2 hours and up to 12 hours. (The longer it cooks, the more flavor you will get.)
3. Carefully pour the mixture through a fine mesh strainer into a large bowl. Taste and season with salt.
4. Serve hot.

Ginger, Mushroom & Cauliflower Broth

Serves: 3   Prep: 10 mins.   Cook: 50 mins.

Nutrition per Serving:
141 calories, 5 g fat, 22 g carbs, 7 g fiber, 5 g protein

Ingredients:

- 1 large yellow onion
- 1 cup celery stalks chopped
- 2 carrots diced or cubed
- 10 French beans
- 1 ginger root, peeled and diced or grated
- 1 to 2 stalks celery leaves or coriander leaves

- 1½ cup mushrooms sliced
- 8 florets cauliflower
- 1 tsp garlic chopped
- 1 tbsp oil
- 1 stalk spring onion greens or scallions
- ½ tsp crushed pepper or ground pepper

Directions:

1. Transfer your ingredients to your stockpot. Top with enough water to cover then allow to slowly come to a boil on high heat.
2. Switch to low heat and simmer for at least 50 minutes on low hat.
3. Carefully pour the mixture through a fine mesh strainer into a large bowl. Taste and season with salt.
4. Serve hot. Enjoy!

Fish Broth

Yields: 32   Prep: 15 mins.   Cook: 45 mins.

Nutrition per Serving:

29 calories, 1 g fat, 2 g carbs, 1 g fiber, 1 g protein

Ingredients:

- olive oil (3 tablespoons)
- onion (1 large, chopped)
- carrot (1 large, chopped)
- fennel bulb (1, chopped, optional)
- celery stalks (3, chopped)
- Salt
- white wine (2 cups)
- fish bones and heads (2 to 5 pounds)
- mushrooms (A handful of dried, optional)
- bay leaves (2 to 4)
- 1-star anise pod (optional)
- Thyme (1 to 2 teaspoons dried or fresh)
- kombu kelp (3 or 4 pieces of dried, optional)
- Chopped fronds from the fennel bulb

Directions:

1. Transfer the bones and vegetables to your stockpot. Top with enough water to cover then allow to slowly come to a boil on high heat.
2. Switch to low heat and simmer for 45 mins.
3. Carefully pour the mixture through a fine mesh strainer into a large bowl. Taste and season with salt.
4. Serve hot. Enjoy!

Clear Pumpkin Broth

Yields: 6 cups   Prep: 15 mins.   Cook: 30 mins.
Nutrition per Serving:
216 calories, 1 g fat, 37 g carbs, 4 g fiber, 8 g protein

Ingredients:

- instant dashi powder (3 teaspoons)
- sake or dry sherry (1 cup)
- mirin (2 tablespoons)
- soy sauce (1 cup)
- sugar (2 tablespoons)
- water (6 cups)
- ginger (2 tablespoons, minced)
- potatoes (2 cups, peeled and diced)
- kabocha (3 cups, peeled and diced)
- carrot (1, peeled and diced)
- onion (1, diced)
- scallions (½ cup, chopped)

Directions:
1. Transfer the bones and vegetables to your stockpot. Top with enough water to cover then allow to slowly come to a boil on high heat.
2. Switch to low heat and simmer for at least 30 minutes
3. Carefully pour the mixture through a fine mesh strainer into a large bowl. Taste and season with salt.
4. Serve hot. Enjoy!

Pork Stock

Yields: 8 cups   Prep: 15 mins.   Cook: 12 hours

Nutrition per Serving:
69 calories, 4 g fat, 1 g carbs, 0.1 g fiber, 6 g protein

Ingredients:

- pork bones (2 Pounds, roasted)
- onion (1, chopped in quarters)
- celery stalks (2, chopped in half)
- carrots (2, chopped in half)
- garlic cloves (3, whole)

- bay leaves (2)
- apple cider vinegar (2 Tablespoons)
- salt (1 Tablespoon)
- peppercorns (1/2 Tablespoon)
- filtered water (enough to cover bones)

Directions:
1. Transfer the bones and vegetables to your stockpot. Top with enough water to cover then allow to slowly come to a boil on high heat.
2. Switch to low heat and simmer for 12 hours on low. (The longer it cooks, the more flavor you will get.)
3. Carefully pour the mixture through a fine mesh strainer into a large bowl. Taste and season with salt.
4. Serve hot. Enjoy!

Slow Cooker Pork Bone Broth

Yields: 12 cups   Prep: 15 mins.   Cook: 24 hours + roasting time

Nutrition per Serving:
65 calories, 2 g fat, 7 g carbs, 4 g fiber, 6 g protein

Ingredients:

- pork bones (2 pounds – roasted)
- onion (½ chopped)
- carrots (2 medium chopped)
- celery (1 stalk chopped)
- garlic whole (2 cloves)

- bay leaf (1)
- sea salt (1 tablespoon)
- peppercorns (1 teaspoon)
- Apple Cider Vinegar (¼ cup)
- Filtered water

Directions

1. Transfer your ingredients to your slow cooker. Top with enough water to cover then allow to slowly come to a boil on high heat.
2. Switch to low heat and simmer for at least 24 hours on low. (The longer it cooks, the more flavor you will get.)
3. Carefully pour the mixture through a fine mesh strainer into a large bowl. Taste and season with salt.
4. Serve hot. Enjoy!

Pulpless Fruit & Vegetable Juices

Homemade No Pulp Orange Juice

Yields: 1 ½ cups   Prep: 5 mins.   Cook: 0 mins.

Nutrition per Serving:
50 calories, 0.2 g fat, 11.5 g carbs, g fiber, 0.8 g protein

Ingredients:

- Oranges (4)

Directions:

1. Lightly squeeze the oranges on a hard surface to soften the exterior. Slice each in half.
2. Squeeze each orange over a fine mesh strainer.
3. Gently press the pulp to extract all possible liquid.
4. Serve over ice. Enjoy!

Apple Orange Juice

Yields: 2   Prep: 5 mins.   Cook: 0 mins.

Nutrition per Serving:

180 calories, 1 g fat, 43 g carbs, 1 g fiber, 2 g protein

Ingredients:

- ❖ Apple (1 Gala, peeled, cored, sliced)
- ❖ Oranges (2, peeled, halved, seeded)
- ❖ Honey (2 tsp, optional)
- ❖ Water (3/4 cup)

Directions:

1. Squeeze each orange over a fine mesh strainer.
2. Gently press the pulp to extract as much liquid as possible.
3. Add in your apple, water, and orange juice in your blender and blend.
4. Set a fine mesh strainer a bowl. Before transferring your juice into the strainer.
5. Once again, gently press the pulp to remove all possible liquid then discard pulp.
6. Stir in your honey then serve over ice.

Pineapple Mint Juice

Yields: 4   Prep: 5 mins.   Cook: 0 mins.

Nutrition per Serving:

78 calories, 1 g fat, 22 g carbs, 2 g fiber, 1 g protein

Ingredients:
- pineapple (3 cups, cored and sliced, chunks)
- mint leaves (10 to 12, or to taste)
- sugar, or to taste (2 tablespoons, optional)
- water (1 1/2 cups)
- ice cubes (1 cup)

Directions:
1. Add all your ingredients into your blender, and blend.
2. Set a fine mesh strainer a bowl. Before transferring your juice into the strainer.
3. Gently press the pulp to extract all possible liquid then discard pulp.
4. Serve over ice. Enjoy!

Homemade Banana Apple Juice

Serves: 2   Prep: 10 mins.   Cook: 0 mins.

Nutrition per Serving:

132 calories, 2 g fat, 27 g carbs, 3 g fiber, 4 g protein

Ingredients:
- Bananas (2, peeled, sliced)
- Apple (1/2, peeled, cored and chopped)
- Honey (1 tbsp.)
- Water (1½ cups)

Directions:
1. Add all your ingredients into your blender, and blend.
2. Set a fine mesh strainer a bowl. Before transferring your juice into the strainer.
3. Gently press the pulp to extract all possible liquid then discard pulp.
4. Serve over ice. Enjoy!

Sweet Detox Juice

Yields: 2 serving   Prep: 10 mins.   Cook: 0 mins.
Nutrition per Serving:
209 calories, 2 g fat, 48 g carbs, 17 g fiber, 12 g protein

Ingredients:
- ❖ baby spinach (2 cups, chopped)
- ❖ parsley (1 handful, chopped)
- ❖ apple (1, green, peeled, cored, seeded, sliced0

- ❖ cucumber (1 large English, seeded, chopped)
- ❖ ginger (1-inch, peeled)
- ❖ lemon (1, juiced)

Directions:
1. Add all your ingredients into your blender, and blend.
2. Set a fine mesh strainer a bowl. Before transferring your juice into the strainer.
3. Gently press the pulp to extract all possible liquid then discard pulp.
4. Serve over ice. Enjoy!

Pineapple Ginger Juice

Yields: 7 cups   Prep: 35 mins.   Cook: 0 mins.
Nutrition per Serving:
71 calories, 1 g fat, 20 g carbs, 3 g fiber, 1 g protein

Ingredients:
- pineapple (10 cups, chopped)
- water (6 cups)
- Apples (3, Fuji, chopped)

- ginger (4-inch root, peeled, chopped)
- lemon juice (1/4 cup)
- sugar (1/4 cup)

Directions:
1. Add all your ingredients into your blender, and blend.
2. Set a fine mesh strainer a bowl. Before transferring your juice into the strainer.
3. Gently press the pulp to extract all possible liquid then discard pulp.
4. Serve over ice. Enjoy!

Tropical Fruit Punch

Yields: 4 glasses   Prep: 3 mins.   Cook: 0 mins.
Nutrition per Serving:
247 calories, 1 g fat, 65 g carbs, 10 g fiber, 3 g protein

Ingredients:
- Pineapple (1, peeled, cored, sliced)
- Apples (2, peeled, cored, quartered)
- Oranges (2, juiced)
- Pears (2, peeled, seeded, quartered)
- Lime (1, juiced)
- Water (2 cups)

Directions:
1. Add all your ingredients into your blender, and blend.
2. Set a fine mesh strainer a bowl. Before transferring your juice into the strainer.
3. Gently press the pulp to extract all possible liquid then discard pulp.
4. Serve over ice. Enjoy!

Carrot Orange Juice

Yields: 2 servings   Prep: 15 mins.   Cook: 0 mins.
Nutrition per Serving:
111 calories, 1 g fat, 24 g carbs, 1 g fiber, 2 g protein

Ingredients:
- Tomato (1, yellow, medium), cut into wedges
- Orange (1, peeled, quartered)
- Apple (1, peeled, cored, chopped)
- Carrots (4, jumbo, peeled, chopped)
- Water (2 cups)

Directions:
1. Add all your ingredients into your blender, and blend.
2. Set a fine mesh strainer a bowl. Before transferring your juice into the strainer.
3. Gently press the pulp to extract all possible liquid then discard pulp.
4. Serve over ice. Enjoy!

Strawberry Apple Juice

Yields: 8-10 oz   Prep: 5 mins.   Cook: 0 mins.
Nutrition per Serving:
245 calories, 5 g fat, 52 g carbs, 7 g fiber, 4 g protein

Ingredients:
- ❖ Strawberries (2 cups, tops removed)
- ❖ Apple (1, red, peeled, seeded, cored, chopped)
- ❖ chia seeds (1 tbsp.)
- ❖ Water (1 cup)

Directions:
1. Add all your ingredients into your blender, and blend.
2. Set a fine mesh strainer a bowl. Before transferring your juice into the strainer.
3. Gently press the pulp to extract all possible liquid then discard pulp.
4. Add in your chia seeds then leave to sit for at least 5 minutes.
5. Serve over ice. Enjoy!

Autumn Energizer Juice

Yields: 2 serving   Prep: 10 mins.   Cook: 0 mins.
Nutrition per Serving:
170 calories, 3 g fat, 33 g carbs, 9 g fiber, 4 g protein

Ingredients:
- ❖ Pears (2, peeled, seeded, chopped)
- ❖ Apples (2, Ambrosia, peeled, cored, chopped)
- ❖ Apples (2, Granny Smith, peeled, cored, chopped)
- ❖ Mandarins (2, juiced)
- ❖ sweet potato (2 cups, peeled, chopped)
- ❖ cape gooseberries (1 pint)
- ❖ ginger (2-inch root, peeled)

Directions:
1. Add all your ingredients into your blender, and blend.
2. Set a fine mesh strainer a bowl. Before transferring your juice into the strainer.
3. Gently press the pulp to extract all possible liquid then discard pulp.
4. Serve over ice. Enjoy!

Pineapple Ice Cubes

Yields: 24 ice cubes   Prep: 4 hrs. 10 mins.   Cook: 0 mins.
Nutrition per Serving:
70 calories, 0 g fat, 18 g carbs, 2 g fiber, 1 g protein

Ingredients:

❖ Pineapple Juice (3 cups, unsweetened).

Directions:
1. Fill your empty ice trays with your juice.
2. Set to freeze for at least 3 hours until frozen.
3. Transfer your flavored ice cubes to freezer bags.
4. Keep them in the freezer until ready to serve.

Gala Apple Flavored Ice Cubes

Yields: 24 ice cubes   Prep: 4 hrs. 10 mins.   Cook: 0 mins.
Nutrition per Serving:
83 calories, 1 g fat, 21 g carbs, 2 g fiber, 1 g protein

Ingredients:

❖ Apple (2, Gala)
❖ Honey (4 tsp.)

❖ Water (3 cups)

Directions:
1. Add all your ingredients into your blender, and blend.
2. Set a fine mesh strainer a bowl. Before transferring your juice into the strainer.
3. Gently press the pulp to extract all possible liquid then discard pulp.
4. Fill your empty ice trays with your juice.
5. Set to freeze for at least 3 hours until frozen.
6. Transfer your flavored ice cubes to freezer bags.
7. Keep them in the freezer until ready to serve.

Iced Tea Ice Cubes

Yields: 24 ice cubes   Prep: 4 hrs. 10 mins.   Cook: 0 mins.
Nutrition per Serving:
20 calories, 0 g fat, 3 g carbs, 0 g fiber, 0 g protein

Ingredients:

- ❖ Iced Tea (3 cups, unsweetened)

Directions:
1. Fill your empty ice trays with your juice.
2. Set to freeze for at least 3 hours until frozen.
3. Transfer your flavored ice cubes to freezer bags.
4. Keep them in the freezer until ready to serve.

Celery Pine Ice Cubes

Yields: 24 ice cubes   Prep: 4 hrs. 10mins.   Cook: 0 mins.
Nutrition per Serving:
160 calories, 12 g fat, 11 g carbs, 0 g fiber, 2 g protein

Ingredients:

- ❖ Pineapple (2 cups, chopped)
- ❖ Water (3 cups)
- ❖ celery (4 stalks, peeled, chopped)

Directions:
1. Add all your ingredients into your blender, and blend.
2. Set a fine mesh strainer a bowl. Before transferring your juice into the strainer.
3. Gently press the pulp to extract all possible liquid then discard pulp.
4. Fill your empty ice trays with your juice.
5. Set to freeze for at least 3 hours until frozen.
6. Transfer your flavored ice cubes to freezer bags.
7. Keep them in the freezer until ready to serve.

Kale Flavored Ice Cubes

Yields: 24 ice cubes   Prep: 4 hrs. 10 mins.   Cook: 0 mins.

Nutrition per Serving:

110 calories, 1 g fat, 25 g carbs, 4 g fiber, 3 g protein

Ingredients:

- ❖ Honey (¼ cup)
- ❖ Water (2 cups)
- ❖ Kale (3 cups, chopped)

Directions:
1. Add all your ingredients into your blender, and blend.
2. Set a fine mesh strainer a bowl. Before transferring your juice into the strainer.
3. Gently press the pulp to extract all possible liquid then discard pulp.
4. Fill your empty ice trays with your juice.
5. Set to freeze for at least 3 hours until frozen.
6. Transfer your flavored ice cubes to freezer bags.
7. Keep them in the freezer until ready to serve.

Cranberry Flavored Ice Cubes

Yields: 24 ice cubes   Prep: 4 hrs. 10 mins.   Cook: 0 mins.
Nutrition per Serving:
120 calories, 2 g fat, 24g carbs, 1 g fiber, 0 g protein

Ingredients:

   ❖ Cranberry Juice (3 cups, unsweetened)

Directions:
1. Fill your empty ice trays with your juice.
2. Set to freeze for at least 3 hours until frozen.
3. Transfer your flavored ice cubes to freezer bags.
4. Keep them in the freezer until ready to serve.

Cucumber Flavored Ice Cubes

Yields: 24 ice cubes   Prep: 4 hrs. 10 mins.   Cook: 0 mins.
Nutrition per Serving:
6 calories, 0 g fat, g carbs, 2 g fiber, 0 g protein

Ingredients:

   ❖ Honey (¼ cup)   ❖ Cucumber (3 cups, chopped)
   ❖ Water (2 cups)

Directions:
1. Add all your ingredients into your blender, and blend.
2. Set a fine mesh strainer a bowl. Before transferring your juice into the strainer.
3. Gently press the pulp to extract all possible liquid then discard pulp.
4. Fill your empty ice trays with your juice.
5. Set to freeze for at least 3 hours until frozen.
6. Transfer your flavored ice cubes to freezer bags.
7. Keep them in the freezer until ready to serve.

Mango Flavored Ice Cubes

Yields: 24 ice cubes   Prep: 4 hrs. 10 mins.   Cook: 0 mins.

Nutrition per Serving:

5 calories, 0 g fat, 2 g carbs, 0 g fiber, 0 g protein

Ingredients:
- ❖ Honey (¼ cup)
- ❖ Water (2 cups)
- ❖ Mango (3 cups, peeled and chopped)

Directions:
1. Add all your ingredients into your blender, and blend.
2. Set a fine mesh strainer a bowl. Before transferring your juice into the strainer.
3. Gently press the pulp to extract all possible liquid then discard pulp.
4. Fill your empty ice trays with your juice.
5. Set to freeze for at least 3 hours until frozen.
6. Transfer your flavored ice cubes to freezer bags.
7. Keep them in the freezer until ready to serve.

Banana Ice Cubes

Yields: 24 ice cubes   Prep: 15 mins.   Cook: 0 mins.

Nutrition per Serving:

71 calories, 0 g fat, 16 g carbs, 1 g fiber, 2 g protein

Ingredients:

- ❖ Bananas (2, peeled, sliced)
- ❖ Honey (1 tbsp.)
- ❖ Water (3 cups)

Directions:

1. Add all your ingredients into your blender, and blend.
2. Set a fine mesh strainer a bowl. Before transferring your juice into the strainer.
3. Gently press the pulp to extract all possible liquid then discard pulp.
4. Fill your empty ice trays with your juice.
5. Set to freeze for at least 3 hours until frozen.
6. Transfer your flavored ice cubes to freezer bags.
7. Keep them in the freezer until ready to serve.

Apple Flavored Ice Cubes

Yields: 24 ice cubes   Prep: 4hrs. 10 mins.   Cook: 0 mins.

Nutrition per Serving:

38 calories, 0 g fat, 12 g carbs, 1 g fiber, 0 g protein

Ingredients:

- Apple Juice (3 cups, unsweetened)

Directions:

1. Fill your empty ice trays with your juice.
2. Set to freeze for at least 3 hours until frozen.
3. Transfer your flavored ice cubes to freezer bags.
4. Keep them in the freezer until ready to serve.

Pineapple Ginger Ice Cubes

Yields: 24 ice cubes   Prep: 4 hrs. 10 mins.   Cook: 0 mins.

Nutrition per Serving:

172 calories, 0 g fat, 19 g carbs, 0 g fiber, 0 g protein

Ingredients:

- ❖ Pineapple Ginger Juice (3 cups)

Directions:
1. Fill your empty ice trays with your juice.
2. Set to freeze for at least 3 hours until frozen.
3. Transfer your flavored ice cubes to freezer bags.
4. Keep them in the freezer until ready to serve.

Clear Ice Pops
Blackberry-Rose Ice Pops

Yields: 10   Prep: 25 mins.   Cook: 5 hrs.
Nutrition per Serving:
112 calories, 0 g fat, 30g carbs, 5 g fiber, 1 g protein

Ingredients:
- ❖ cane sugar (9 tbsp., organic)
- ❖ Water (9 tbsp., for simple syrup)
- ❖ blackberries (6 1/2 cups)
- ❖ lemon juice (1 tbsp.)
- ❖ rosewater (1 tsp.)
- ❖ Water (1 cup)

Directions:
1. Create a simple syrup by heating sugar and the water for the simple syrup over medium heat.
2. Allow the mixture to simmer, stirring until the sugar dissolves. Set to cool (about 10 minutes).
3. Add all your ingredients into your blender, and blend.
4. Set a fine mesh strainer a bowl. Before transferring your juice into the strainer.
5. Gently press the pulp to extract all possible liquid then discard pulp.
6. Pour your juice into your ice-pop molds, filling each three quarters of the way.
7. Add in your ice pop sticks then set to freeze for at least 5 hours or until solid. Unmold and enjoy.

Frozen Strawberry-Peach Pops

Yields: 5   Prep: 5 mins.   Cook: 0 mins.

Nutrition per Serving:

102 calories, 1 g fat, 12g carbs, 2 g fiber, 2 g protein

Ingredients:

- ❖ Sugar (1/2 cup)
- ❖ Strawberries (6 oz.)
- ❖ Peaches (6 oz.)

- ❖ Water (4 oz.)
- ❖ Lemon Juice (1 tbsp.)

Directions:

1. Create a simple syrup by heating sugar and water over medium heat.
2. Allow the mixture to simmer, stirring until the sugar dissolves. Set to cool (about 10 minutes).
3. Add all your ingredients into your blender, and blend.
4. Set a fine mesh strainer a bowl. Before transferring your juice into the strainer.
5. Gently press the pulp to extract all possible liquid then discard pulp.
6. Pour your juice into your ice-pop molds, filling each three quarters of the way.
7. Add in your ice pop sticks then set to freeze for at least 5 hours or until solid. Unmold and enjoy.

Honey Lemonade Popsicles

Yields: 8   Prep: 5 mins.   Cook: 0 mins.

Nutrition per Serving:

36 calories, 3 g fat, 3 g carbs, 1g fiber, 3 g protein

Ingredients:

- Honey (1/2 cup)
- Lemon Juice (12 oz.)
- Water (6 oz.)

Directions:
1. Create honey water by heating honey and over medium heat.
2. Allow the mixture to simmer, stirring until the honey melts. Set to cool (about 10 minutes).
3. In a spouted container, combine all your ingredients.
4. Pour your juice into your ice-pop molds, filling each three quarters of the way.
5. Add in your ice pop sticks then set to freeze for at least 5 hours or until solid. Unmold and enjoy.

Orange Strawberry Popsicles

Yields: 12 popsicles   Prep: 10 mins.   Cook: 0 mins.

Nutrition per Serving:

160 calories, 0 g fat, 40 g carbs, 1 g fiber, 0 g protein

Ingredients:

- Strawberry (4 cups, hulled)
- orange juice (2 cups)
- lime (1, juiced)
- Honey (1/4 cup)

Directions:
1. Add all your ingredients into your blender, and blend.
2. Set a fine mesh strainer a bowl. Before transferring your juice into the strainer.
3. Gently press the pulp to extract all possible liquid then discard pulp.
4. Pour your juice into your ice-pop molds, filling each three quarters of the way.

Melon Basil Moscow Mule Popsicles

Yields: 10 popsicles   Prep: 5 mins.   Cook: 0 mins.

Nutrition per Serving:

34 calories, 0 g fat, 8 g carbs, 1 g fiber, 2 g protein

Ingredients:

- Cantaloupe (1 lb., peeled, seeded chopped)
- Mint (7 leaves)
- Water (4 oz.)

- Limeade (4 oz.)
- Ginger Beer (16 oz.)
- Simple Syrup (2 oz.)

Directions:

1. Add all your ingredients into your blender, and blend.
2. Set a fine mesh strainer a bowl. Before transferring your juice into the strainer.
3. Gently press the pulp to extract all possible liquid then discard pulp.
4. Pour your juice into your ice-pop molds, filling each three quarters of the way.

Honeydew Mint Homemade Popsicles

Yields: 10 popsicles   Prep: 10 mins.   Cook: 0 mins.
Nutrition per Serving:
34 calories, 0 g fat, 8 g carbs, 1 g fiber, 2 g protein

Ingredients:
- Honeydew melon (1/2, peeled, cubed)
- Granulated sugar (1/3 cup)
- Mint (10 leaves)
- Lime juice (1 tbsp.)
- Water (6 oz.)
- xanthan gum (1 pinch)

Directions:
1. Add all your ingredients into your blender, and blend.
2. Set a fine mesh strainer a bowl. Before transferring your juice into the strainer.
3. Gently press the pulp to extract all possible liquid then discard pulp.
4. Pour your juice into your ice-pop molds, filling each three quarters of the way.

Raspberry Lemonade Popsicles

Yields: 10 popsicle Prep: 5 mins.   Cook: 0 mins.
Nutrition per Serving:
43 calories, 1 g fat, 6 g carbs, 1 g fiber, 4 g protein

Ingredients:
- lemonade concentrate (2 cup)
- lemon-lime soda (48 oz.)
- Fresh raspberries (1 pint)

Directions:
1. Add all your ingredients into your blender, and blend.
2. Set a fine mesh strainer a bowl. Before transferring your juice into the strainer.
3. Gently press the pulp to extract all possible liquid then discard pulp.
4. Pour your juice into your ice-pop molds, filling each three quarters of the way.

Strawberry Popsicles

Yields: 12 popsicle Prep: 10 mins.   Cook: 0 mins.
Nutrition per Serving:
60 calories, 1 g fat, 15 g carbs, 1 g fiber, 2 g protein

Ingredients:
- Strawberries (4 cups, hulled)
- Water (2 cups)
- Lime (1, juiced)
- Honey (1/4 cup)

Directions:
1. Create a simple syrup by heating sugar and water over medium heat.
2. Allow the mixture to simmer, stirring until the sugar dissolves. Set to cool (about 10 minutes).
3. Add all your ingredients into your blender, and blend.
4. Set a fine mesh strainer a bowl. Before transferring your juice into the strainer.
5. Gently press the pulp to extract all possible liquid then discard pulp.
6. Pour your juice into your ice-pop molds, filling each three quarters of the way.

Basil Watermelon Popsicles

Yields: 12 popsicle Prep: 10 mins.   Cook: 0 mins.
Nutrition per Serving:
47 calories, 0 g fat, 12 g carbs, 1 g fiber, 1 g protein

Ingredients:
- Watermelon (1 lb.)
- Basil (5 leaves)
- Water (12 oz.)
- Lime Juice (4 oz.)
- Honey (1 oz.)

Directions:
1. Create honey water by heating honey and over medium heat.
2. Allow the mixture to simmer, stirring until the honey melts. Set to cool (about 10 minutes).
3. In a spouted container, combine all your ingredients.
4. Pour your juice into your ice-pop molds, filling each three quarters of the way.
5. Add in your ice pop sticks then set to freeze for at least 5 hours or until solid. Unmold and enjoy.

Orange Popsicles

Yields: 12 popsicle Prep: 10 mins.   Cook: 0 mins.
Nutrition per Serving:
121 calories, 0 g fat, 12 g carbs, 1 g fiber, 0 g protein

Ingredients:
- orange juice (3 cups)
- lime (1, juiced)

Directions:
1. Set a fine mesh strainer a bowl. Before transferring your juice into the strainer.
2. Gently press the pulp to extract all possible liquid then discard pulp.
3. Pour your juice into your ice-pop molds, filling each three quarters of the way.

Grapefruit Lemonade Popsicles

Yields: 8 popsicle   Prep: 10 mins.   Cook: 0 mins.
Nutrition per Serving:
71 calories, 0.1 g fat, 17.3 g carbs, 0.1 g fiber, 0.3 g protein

Ingredients:
- ❖ Honey (1/4 cup)
- ❖ Grapefruit Juice (2½ cup)
- ❖ Lemon Juice (12 oz.)
- ❖ Water (6 oz.)

Directions:
1. Create honey water by heating honey and over medium heat.
2. Allow the mixture to simmer, stirring until the honey melts. Set to cool (about 10 minutes).
3. In a spouted container, combine all your ingredients.
4. Pour your juice into your ice-pop molds, filling each three quarters of the way.
5. Add in your ice pop sticks then set to freeze for at least 5 hours or until solid. Unmold and enjoy.

Gelatin
3-Ingredient Sugar Free Gelatin

Yields:6-8   Prep: 5 mins.   Cook: 4hrs.
Nutrition per Serving:
17 calories, 0 g fat, 4 g carbs, 0 g fiber, 0 g protein

Ingredients:

- ❖ Water (1/4 cup, room temperature)
- ❖ Water (1/4 cup, hot)
- ❖ Gelatin (1 tbsp.)
- ❖ Orange Juice (1 cup, unsweetened)

Directions:
1. Combine your gelatin and room temperature water, stirring until fully dissolved.
2. Stir in your hot water then leave to rest for about 2 minutes.
3. Add in your juice and stir until combined.
4. Transfer to serving size containers then place on a tray in the refrigerator to set for about 4 hours.
5. Enjoy!

Cran - Kombucha Jell-O

Yields: 6   Prep: 5 mins.   Cook: 4hrs.
Nutrition per Serving:
13 calories, 0 g fat, 1 g carbs, 0 g fiber, 0 g protein

Ingredients:
- ❖ Water (1/4 cup, room temperature)
- ❖ Hot Water (1/4 cup)
- ❖ Gelatin (1 tbsp.)
- ❖ Cranberry kombucha (1 cup, unsweetened)

Directions:
1. Combine your gelatin and room temperature water, stirring until fully dissolved.
2. Stir in your hot water then leave to rest for about 2 minutes.
3. Add in your kombucha and stir until combined.
4. Transfer to serving size containers then place on a tray in the refrigerator to set for about 4 hours.
5. Enjoy!

Strawberry Gummies

Yields: 20-40 mini gummies   Prep: 5 mins.   Cook: 4 hrs.
Nutrition per Serving:
3 calories, 0 g fat, 0 g carbs, 0 g fiber, 0 g protein

Ingredients:
- ❖ Strawberries (1 cup, hulled, chopped)
- ❖ Water (3/4 cup)
- ❖ Gelatin (2 tbsp.)

Directions:
1. Set your water and berries on to boil on high heat. /remove from heat as soon as the mixture begins to boil.
2. Transfer to your blender and blend. Add in your gelatin then blend once more.
3. Pour your mixture into a silicone gummy mold.
4. Place on a tray in the refrigerator to set for about 4 hours.
5. Enjoy!

Elderberry Gummies

Yields: 20-50 Prep: 7 mins.   Cook: 4 hrs.
Nutrition per Serving:
3 calories, 0 g fat, 1 g carbs, 0 g fiber, 0 g protein

Ingredients:
- Gelatin (2 tbsp.)
- Water (1/4 cup, room temperature)
- Hot Water (1/4 cup)
- Orange Juice (1/2 cup)
- Lemon Juice (2 tbsp.)
- Elderberry Soothing Syrup (2 tbsp.)

Directions:
1. Combine your gelatin and room temperature water, stirring until fully dissolved.
2. Stir in your hot water then leave to rest for about 2 minutes.
3. Add in your remaining ingredients and stir until combined.
4. Transfer to serving size containers then place on a tray in the refrigerator to set for about 4 hours.
5. Enjoy!

Fruity Jell-O Stars

Yields: 4   Prep: 15 mins.   Cook: 5 mins.
Nutrition per Serving:
73 calories, 2 g fat, 14 g carbs, 0 g fiber, 1 g protein

Ingredients:
- ❖ Gelatin (1 Tbsp, powdered)
- ❖ Boiling Water (3/4 cup)
- ❖ Fruit (3 ½ cups)
- ❖ Honey (1 Tbsp)
- ❖ Lemon Juice (1 Tsp.)

Directions:
1. Add all your ingredients into your blender and blend. Add in your gelatin then blend once more.
2. Pour your mixture into a silicone gummy mold.
3. Place on a tray in the refrigerator to set for about 4 hours.
4. Enjoy!

Ginger Beer Gelatin Dessert

Yields: 8 serving   Prep: 5 mins.   Cook: 3 hrs.
Nutrition per Serving:
67 calories, 0 g fat, 6 g carbs, 1 g fiber, 1 g protein

Ingredients:
- ❖ Raspberries (2 cups, chopped)
- ❖ Water (1 cup)
- ❖ Gelatin (2 tbsp.)
- ❖ Ginger Beer (1 1/2 cups)
- ❖ Lemon Juice (1 tbsp.)
- ❖ Stevia to taste, if desired

Directions:
1. Stir your gelatin into your water then set it to rest in a saucepan for about 5 minutes.
2. Set to heat up on low heat until glossy and lump free.
3. Combine all your remaining ingredients then slowly stir in your gelatin mix.
4. Transfer to molds then set to refrigerate for about 4 hours or until set. Enjoy!

Plum and Nectarine Gelatin Pudding

Yields: 5   Prep: 15 mins.   Cook: 0 mins.

Nutrition per Serving:

157 calories, 5g fat, 26 g carbs, 1 g fiber, 3 g protein

Ingredients:

- ❖ Nectarine (1, large)
- ❖ Plums (2, small)
- ❖ Gelatin (2 tbsp.)
- ❖ Water (1 1/2 cup, room temp.)

- ❖ Boiling water (2 cups)
- ❖ lemon juice (2 tsp.)
- ❖ Honey (1/3 cup)
- ❖ Vanilla (1 tsp.)
- ❖ sea salt (1/8 tsp.)

Directions:

1. Add your fruits in your blend to puree until smooth with room temperature water, lemon juice and vanilla until smooth.
2. Strain through a fine mesh strainer.
3. Combine your gelatin and fruit mixture, stirring until fully dissolved.
4. Stir in your hot water then leave to rest for about 2 minutes.
5. Add in your remaining ingredients and stir until combined.
6. Transfer to serving size containers then place on a tray in the refrigerator to set for about 4 hours.
7. Enjoy!

Homemade Lemon Gelatin

Yields: 8   Prep: 2 hrs. 5 mins.   Cook: 0 mins.

Nutrition per Serving:

68 calories, 0 g fat, 1 g carbs, 0 g fiber, 2 g protein

Ingredients:

- ❖ Gelatin (3 tbsp., granulated)
- ❖ Stevia (1½ cup)
- ❖ Boiling Water (1 1/2 cups)
- ❖ Cold Water (3 cups)
- ❖ Lemon Juice (1 1/8 cups)
- ❖ Lemon zest (1/2 tsp)

Directions:

1. Combine your gelatin and room temperature water, stirring until fully dissolved.
2. Stir in your hot water then leave to rest for about 2 minutes.
3. Add in your remaining ingredients and stir until combined.
4. Transfer to serving size containers then place on a tray in the refrigerator to set for about 4 hours.
5. Enjoy!

Sugar – Free Cinnamon Jelly

Yields: 2   Prep: 2 hrs. 15 mins.   Cook: 0 mins.

Nutrition per Serving:

35 calories, 0 g fat, 17 g carbs, 0 g fiber, 0 g protein

Ingredients:

- ❖ Hot Herbal Tea (1 cup)
- ❖ Room Temperature Water (1 cup)
- ❖ Gelatin (2 tsp)
- ❖ Sweetener (⅓ cup)

Directions:

1. Combine your gelatin and room temperature water, stirring until fully dissolved.
2. Stir in your hot water then leave to rest for about 2 minutes.
3. Add in your juice and stir until combined.
4. Transfer to serving size containers then place on a tray in the refrigerator to set for about 4 hours.
5. Enjoy!

Sour Blueberry Gummies

Yields: 9   Prep: 5 mins.   Cook: 5 mins.

Nutrition per Serving:

73 calories, 2 g fat, 14 g carbs, 0 g fiber, 1 g protein

Ingredients:

- Blueberries (1 1/2 cup)
- lemon juice (1 cup)
- honey (3 tbsp)
- gelatin (1/3 cup, grass-fed)

Directions:

1. Set your water and berries on to boil on high heat. /remove from heat as soon as the mixture begins to boil.
2. Transfer to your blender and blend. Add in your gelatin then blend once more.
3. Pour your mixture into a silicone gummy mold.
4. Place on a tray in the refrigerator to set for about 4 hours.
5. Enjoy!

Homemade Orange Gelatin

Yields: 8   Prep: 2 hrs. 5 mins. Cook: 0 mins.

Nutrition per Serving:

68 calories, 0 g fat, 1 g carbs, 0 g fiber, 2 g protein

Ingredients:

- gelatin (3 Tbsp, granulated)
- stevia extract (1 cup)
- boiling water (1 1/2 cups)
- cold water (3 cups)
- orange juice (1 1/8 cup)
- orange zest (1/2 tsp.)

Directions:

1. Combine your gelatin and room temperature water, stirring until fully dissolved.
2. Stir in your hot water then leave to rest for about 2 minutes.
3. Add in your remaining ingredients and stir until combined.
4. Transfer to serving size containers then place on a tray in the refrigerator to set for about 4 hours.
5. Enjoy!

Kiwi Cinnamon Tea

Yields: 4   Prep: 5 mins.   Cook: 25 mins.
<u>Nutrition per Serving:</u>
101 calories, 1 g fat, 27 g carbs, 1 g fiber, 1 g protein

Ingredients:
- ❖ Kiwi (1 cup, chopped)
- ❖ cinnamon sticks (3)
- ❖ water (1-quart)
- ❖ Earl Grey tea (2 bags)
- ❖ Honey (⅓ cup)

Directions:
1. In a large saucepan over high heat, add in the Kiwi, cinnamon sticks, and water then boil.
2. Switch to medium heat and simmer for 15 minutes. Switch off the heat and add the tea bags. Steep for 10 minutes.
3. Using a slotted spoon, remove the solid ingredients. Add the honey and stir well. Add more honey, if desired.
4. Serve hot. If there are any leftovers, store in an airtight container in the refrigerator for up to 5 days. Can be served cold or reheat in the microwave for 1 minute until hot.

Cranberry Green Tea

Yields: 4   Prep: 5 mins.   Cook: 25 mins.

Nutrition per Serving:

95 calories, 0 g fat, 26 g carbs, 1 g fiber, 1 g protein

Ingredients:

- Cranberry (½ cup)
- water (1-quart)
- green tea (2 bags)
- honey (⅓ cup)

Directions:

1. In a large saucepan over high heat, add in the cranberries, and water then boil.
2. Switch to medium heat and simmer for 15 minutes. Switch off the heat and add the tea bags. Steep for 10 minutes.
3. Using a slotted spoon, remove the solid ingredients. Add the honey and stir well. Add more honey, if desired.
4. Serve hot. If there are any leftovers, store in an airtight container in the refrigerator for up to 5 days. Can be served cold or reheat in the microwave for 1 minute until hot.

Cinnamon Orange Tea

Yields: 4   Prep: 5 mins.   Cook: 25 mins.
Nutrition per Serving:
101 calories, 1 g fat, 27 g carbs, 1 g fiber, 1 g protein

Ingredients:
- ❖ orange (1 cup, wedges)
- ❖ cinnamon (3 sticks)
- ❖ water (1-quart)
- ❖ Earl Grey tea (2 bags)
- ❖ Honey (⅓ cup)

Directions:
1. In a large saucepan over high heat, add in the orange, cinnamon sticks, and water then boil.
2. Switch to medium heat and simmer for 15 minutes. Switch off the heat and add the tea bags. Steep for 10 minutes.
3. Using a slotted spoon, remove the solid ingredients. Add the honey and stir well. Add more honey, if desired.
4. Serve hot. If there are any leftovers, store in an airtight container in the refrigerator for up to 5 days. Can be served cold or reheat in the microwave for 1 minute until hot.

Cantaloupe Green Tea

Yields: 4   Prep: 5 mins.   Cook: 25 mins.
Nutrition per Serving:
95 calories, 0 g fat, 26 g carbs, 1 g fiber, 1 g protein

Ingredients:
- ❖ cantaloupe (½ cup)
- ❖ water (1-quart)
- ❖ green tea (2 bags)
- ❖ honey (⅓ cup)

Directions:
1. In a large saucepan over high heat, place the cantaloupe and water then bring to a boil.
2. Lower the heat to medium and simmer for 5 minutes. Remove from the heat and add the green tea bags. Steep for 10 minutes.
3. Using a slotted spoon, remove the solid ingredients. Add the honey and stir until it dissolves. Add more honey, if desired.
4. Serve hot. If there are any leftovers, store in an airtight container in the refrigerator for up to 5 days.
5. Can be served cold or reheat in the microwave for 1 minute until hot.

Pineapple Old Spice Tea

Yields: 4   Prep: 5 mins.   Cook: 25 mins.
Nutrition per Serving:
95 calories, 0 g fat, 26 g carbs, 1 g fiber, 1 g protein

Ingredients:
- ½ cup chopped pineapple
- 1-quart water
- 2 old spice tea bags
- ⅓ cup honey, plus more if desired

Directions:
1. In a large saucepan over high heat, place the pineapple and water then bring to a boil.
2. Lower the heat to medium and simmer for 5 minutes. Remove from the heat and add the green tea bags. Steep for 10 minutes.
3. Using a slotted spoon, remove the solid ingredients. Add the honey and stir until it dissolves. Add more honey, if desired.
4. Serve hot. If there are any leftovers, store in an airtight container in the refrigerator for up to 5 days.
5. Can be served cold or reheat in the microwave for 1 minute until hot.

Vanilla Plum Tea

Yields: 4   Prep: 5 mins.   Cook: 25 mins.

Nutrition per Serving:

101 calories, 1 g fat, 27 g carbs, 1 g fiber, 1 g protein

Ingredients:

- ❖ 1 cup chopped plum
- ❖ 3 vanilla sticks, washed and sliced open
- ❖ 1-quart water
- ❖ 2 bags Earl Grey tea (caffeinated or decaffeinated)
- ❖ ⅓ cup honey, plus more if desired

Directions:

1. In a large saucepan over high heat, place the plum, vanilla and water then bring to a boil.
2. Lower the heat to medium and simmer for 5 minutes. Remove from the heat and add the green tea bags. Steep for 10 minutes.
3. Using a slotted spoon, remove the solid ingredients. Add the honey and stir until it dissolves. Add more honey, if desired.
4. Serve hot. If there are any leftovers, store in an airtight container in the refrigerator for up to 5 days.
5. Can be served cold or reheat in the microwave for 1 minute until hot.

Grape Mint Tea

Yields: 4   Prep: 5 mins.   Cook: 25 mins.

Nutrition per Serving:

95 calories, 0 g fat, 26 g carbs, 1 g fiber, 1 g protein

Ingredients:

- Grapes (½ cup)
- Water (1 quart)
- Mint tea (2 bags)
- Honey (1/3 cup)

Directions:

1. In a large saucepan over high heat, place the grape, and water then bring to a boil.
2. Lower the heat to medium and simmer for 5 minutes. Remove from the heat and add the green tea bags. Steep for 10 minutes.
3. Using a slotted spoon, remove the solid ingredients. Add the honey and stir until it dissolves. Add more honey, if desired.
4. Serve hot. If there are any leftovers, store in an airtight container in the refrigerator for up to 5 days.
5. Can be served cold or reheat in the microwave for 1 minute until hot.

Lavender Pear Tea

Yields: 4   Prep: 5 mins.   Cook: 25 mins.

Nutrition per Serving:

95 calories, 0 g fat, 26 g carbs, 1 g fiber, 1 g protein

Ingredients:

- ❖ Pear (½ cup, copped, seeded)
- ❖ Water (1 quart)
- ❖ lavender tea (2 bags)
- ❖ honey (1/3 cup)

Directions:

1. In a large saucepan over high heat, place the pear, and water then bring to a boil.
2. Lower the heat to medium and simmer for 5 minutes. Remove from the heat and add the green tea bags. Steep for 10 minutes.
3. Using a slotted spoon, remove the solid ingredients. Add the honey and stir until it dissolves. Add more honey, if desired.
4. Serve hot. If there are any leftovers, store in an airtight container in the refrigerator for up to 5 days.
5. Can be served cold or reheat in the microwave for 1 minute until hot.

Banana Tea

Yields: 4   Prep: 5 mins.   Cook: 25 mins.

Nutrition per Serving:

101 calories, 1 g fat, 27 g carbs, 1 g fiber, 1 g protein

Ingredients:

- ❖ Banana (1 cup, peeled, chopped)
- ❖ Vanilla (1 stick, beans scraped out)

- ❖ water (1 quart)
- ❖ Earl Grey tea (2 bags)
- ❖ Honey (1/3 cup)

Directions:

1. In a large saucepan over high heat, place the banana and water then bring to a boil.
2. Lower the heat to medium and simmer for 5 minutes. Remove from the heat and add the green tea bags. Steep for 10 minutes.
3. Using a slotted spoon, remove the solid ingredients. Add the honey and stir until it dissolves. Add more honey, if desired.
4. Serve hot. If there are any leftovers, store in an airtight container in the refrigerator for up to 5 days.
5. Can be served cold or reheat in the microwave for 1 minute until hot.

Apple Lemon Ginger Tea

Yields: 4   Prep: 5 mins.   Cook: 25 mins.

Nutrition per Serving:

95 calories, 0 g fat, 26 g carbs, 1 g fiber, 1 g protein

Ingredients:

- ❖ Apple (½ cup, chopped, seeded)
- ❖ Water (1 quart)
- ❖ lemon ginger tea (2 bags)
- ❖ honey (1/3 cup)

Directions:

1. In a large saucepan over high heat, place the apple, and water then bring to a boil.
2. Lower the heat to medium and simmer for 5 minutes. Remove from the heat and add the green tea bags. Steep for 10 minutes.
3. Using a slotted spoon, remove the solid ingredients. Add the honey and stir until it dissolves. Add more honey, if desired.
4. Serve hot. If there are any leftovers, store in an airtight container in the refrigerator for up to 5 days.
5. Can be served cold or reheat in the microwave for 1 minute until hot.

Blueberry Earl Grey Tea

Yields: 4   Prep: 5 mins.   Cook: 25 mins.
Nutrition per Serving:
101 calories, 1 g fat, 27 g carbs, 1 g fiber, 1 g protein

Ingredients:
- ❖ Blueberries (1 cup, chopped)
- ❖ Water (1 quart)
- ❖ Earl Grey tea (2 bags)
- ❖ Honey (1/3 cup)

Directions:
1. In a large saucepan over high heat, place the blueberries and water then bring to a boil.
2. Lower the heat to medium and simmer for 5 minutes. Remove from the heat and add the green tea bags. Steep for 10 minutes.
3. Using a slotted spoon, remove the solid ingredients. Add the honey and stir until it dissolves. Add more honey, if desired.
4. Serve hot. If there are any leftovers, store in an airtight container in the refrigerator for up to 5 days.
5. Can be served cold or reheat in the microwave for 1 minute until hot.

Low Residue Breakfast Ideas

Oatmeal Waffles

Yields: 2-3   Prep: 10 mins.   Cook: 15 mins.

Nutrition per Serving:

404 calories, 7 g fat, 47 g carbs, 6 g fiber, 15 g protein

Ingredients:

- ❖ Quick Oats (1 1/2 cups)
- ❖ White flour (1/2 cup, refined)
- ❖ baking powder (1 tbs)
- ❖ cinnamon (1 tbs)
- ❖ nutmeg (1 tsp)
- ❖ egg (1)
- ❖ banana (1, mashed)
- ❖ honey (1 tbs)
- ❖ milk (1 1/2 cups)
- ❖ cooking spray (Non-stick)

Directions:

1. In a large bowl mix together oatmeal, cinnamon, baking powder, whole wheat flour, and nutmeg. Set aside.
2. In a separate bowl, mix egg, banana, honey, and milk. Mix dry mixture into wet mixture. Preheat waffle iron.
3. Spray with non-stick cooking spray.
4. Pour less than 1/4 cup batter into hot pan for each waffle.
5. Cook until puffy and dry around edges. Turn and cook other side until golden.

Spinach Frittata

Yields: 4   Prep: 10 mins.   Cook: 30 mins.

Nutrition per Serving:

106 calories, 8 g fat, 7 g carbs, 2 g fiber, 3 g protein

Ingredients:

- olive oil (2 tsp)
- red pepper (1 cup, seeded, chopped)
- garlic (1 clove, minced)
- spinach leaves (3 cups, chopped)
- eggs (4, large, beaten)
- salt (1/2 tsp)
- Parmesan cheese (1/4 cup, freshly grated)

Directions:

1. Preheat oven to 350 degrees. In a non-stick oven pan, heat 1 tsp olive oil over medium heat.
2. Cook red peppers and garlic until vegetables are soft (about 10 minutes). In medium bowl, combine eggs and spinach and salt; set aside.
3. Add remaining 1 tsp olive oil into pan with vegetables and add in the egg mixture.
4. Turn the heat to medium and cook for 15 mins. Sprinkle Parmesan cheese over top of mixture and broil for an additional 4 minutes.

Banana and Pear Pita Pockets

Yields: 1   Prep: 5 mins.   Cook: 25 mins.
Nutrition per Serving:
402 calories, 2 g fat, 87 g carbs, 11 g fiber, 14 g protein

Ingredients:

- Banana (1/2 small, peeled, sliced)
- pita bread (1, round, made with refined white flour)
- pear (1/2, small, peeled, seedless, cored, cooked, sliced)
- cottage cheese (1/4 cup, low fat

Directions:
1. Combine banana, pear, and cottage cheese in a small bowl. Slice pita to make a pocket. Fill pita pocket with mixture. Serve.

Pear Pancakes

Yields: 4   Prep: 5 mins.   Cook: 15 mins.
Nutrition per Serving:
174 calories, 2 g fat, 34 g carbs, 2 g fiber, 5 g protein

Ingredients:

- Eggs (2)
- Pear (1 cup, peeled mashed)
- Cinnamon (1 tsp)
- Sugar (2 tsp)
- Refined white flour (1 1/2 cup)
- flour (1/2 cup, whole-wheat)
- baking powder (2 tsp)
- vanilla (2 tsp)
- cooking spray (Non-stick)

Directions:
1. In a medium bowl, beat eggs until fluffy. Add baking powder, cinnamon, vanilla, sugar, flours, and pear, and continue to stir just until smooth. Heat griddle or non-stick pan over medium heat.
2. Spray with non-stick cooking spray. Pour a sizeable amount of batter that you want your pancake to be into the hot pan.
3. Cook pancakes until puffy and dry around edges. Turn and cook other side until golden. Serve pancakes with additional pear if desired.

Ripe Plantain Bran Muffins

Yields: 12   Prep: 10 mins.   Cook: 20 mins.
Nutrition per Serving:
325 calories, 19 g fat, 37 g carbs, 2 g fiber, 3 g protein

Ingredients:

- ❖ Refined Cereal (1 1/2 cups)
- ❖ Milk (2/3 cup, low fat)
- ❖ Eggs (4, large, lightly beaten)
- ❖ canola oil (1/4 cup)
- ❖ ripe plantain (2, medium, mashed, 1 cup)

- ❖ brown sugar (1/2 cup)
- ❖ refined flour (1 cup, white)
- ❖ baking powder (2 tsp)
- ❖ salt (1/2 tsp)

Directions:

1. Preheat oven to 400F degrees. In a large bowl, combine bran cereal and milk and set aside.
2. Add eggs and oil; stir in brown sugar and mashed ripe plantain. In another bowl, combine salt, flour, and baking powder.
3. Add the dry ingredients into the ripe plantain mixture, stir until combined.
4. Pour batter evenly into a paper-lined muffin tins; Bake 18 minutes or until golden-brown and firm. Allow to cool prior to serving.

Easy Breakfast Bran Muffins

Yields: 10   Prep: 10 mins.   Cook: 20 mins.
Nutrition per Serving:
440 calories, 20 g fat, 57 g carbs, 3 g fiber, 9 g protein

Ingredients:

- ❖ Refined cereal (2 cups)
- ❖ brown sugar (1/2 cup)
- ❖ butter (1/2 cup)
- ❖ eggs (2)
- ❖ buttermilk (1/2 quart)

- ❖ white flour (2 1/2 cups, refined)
- ❖ baking soda (2 1/2 tsp)
- ❖ salt (1/2 tsp)

Directions:

1. Preheat oven to 400F degrees. Soak 1 cup cereal in 1 cup boiling water and set aside.
2. In a mixer, cream sugar and butter together until it is fully mixed. Add each egg separate and beat until fluffy. Add buttermilk and soaked cereal mixture.
3. In another bowl, combine salt, flour and baking soda. Add the flour mixture into the batter and ensure not to over mix.
4. Add in remaining 1 cup of cereal. Pour batter evenly into 10 greased or paper-lined muffin tins. Bake 15-20 minutes. Allow to cool prior to serving.

Apple Oatmeal

Yields: 1   Prep: 8 mins.   Cook: 1 mins.
Nutrition per Serving:
295 calories, 7 g fat, 47 g carbs, 5 g fiber, 13 g protein

Ingredients:

- Instant oatmeal (1/2 cup)
- milk or water (3/4 cup)
- apples (1/2 cup, peeled, cooked pureed)
- brown sugar (1 tsp)

Directions:

1. In a microwave-safe bowl, mix oats, milk or water and apples. Cook in microwave on high for 45 seconds.
2. Stir and microwave for another 30 seconds. Sprinkle with brown sugar and add a splash of milk.

Breakfast Burrito Wrap

Yields: 1   Prep: 15 mins.   Cook: 15 mins.
Nutrition per Serving:
355 calories, 2 g fat, 14 g carbs, 4 g fiber, 23 g protein

Ingredients:

- olive oil (1 tbs, extra virgin)
- turkey bacon (2 slices)
- green bell peppers (1/4 cup, seeded and chopped)
- eggs (2, beaten)
- milk (2 tbs)
- salt (1/4 tsp)
- Monterrey Jack cheese (2 tbs, low- fat, grated)
- Tortilla (1, white)

Directions:

1. In a small non-stick pan, heat olive oil on medium heat and cook turkey about 2 minutes until slightly crispy.
2. Add bell peppers and continue to cook until warmed through. In a small bowl beat together egg with milk and salt.
3. Gently stir in your eggs until almost cooked through. Turn the heat down then add the cheese.
4. Cover and continue to cook until cheese have completely melted. Place the mixture on the tortilla and roll it into a burrito.

Zucchini Omelet

Yields: 4   Prep: 15 mins.   Cook: 15 mins.
Nutrition per Serving:
160 calories, 10 g fat, 14 g carbs, 2 g fiber, 6 g protein

Ingredients:

- olive oil (2 tbs, extra virgin)
- zucchini (1, medium, seeded, cubed)
- tomato (1/2 medium, seeded, chopped)
- eggs (4, large)
- milk (1/4 cup)
- salt (1 tsp)
- English muffins (4, whole wheat)

Directions:

1. In a large non-stick pan, heat olive oil over moderate heat. Add zucchini and tomato.
2. Cook vegetables for 5-10 minutes or until they are soft. In a separate bowl, mix eggs and milk and salt.
3. Add egg mixture to pan and stir to cook through, about 5 minutes. Serve with white English muffins.

Coconut Chia Seed Pudding

Yields: 2   Prep: 10 mins.   Cook: 0 mins.
Nutrition per Serving:
223 calories, 12 g fat, 18 g carbs, 2 g fiber, 10 g protein

Ingredients:

- chia seeds (6 tbsp.)
- coconut milk (2 cups, unsweetened)
- Blueberries for topping

Directions:

1. Combine the chia seeds and milk and mix well. Refrigerate overnight. Stir in the berries and serve.

Spiced Oatmeal

Yields: 1   Prep: 5 mins.   Cook: 2 mins.
Nutrition per Serving:
467 calories, 11 g fat, 33 g carbs, 4 g fiber, 6 g protein

Ingredients:
- quick oats (1/3 cup)
- banana (1/2)
- ginger (1/4 tsp., ground)
- cinnamon (1/8 tsp., ground)
- small sprinkle nutmeg ground
- small sprinkle cloves ground
- 1 tbsp. almond butte

Directions:
1. Combine the oats and water. Microwave for 45 seconds, then stir and cook for another 30-45 seconds.
2. Stir in the spices and drizzle on the almond butter before serving.

Breakfast Cereal

Yields: 4   Prep: 5 mins.   Cook: 5 mins.
Nutrition per Serving:
228 calories, 3 g fat, 43 g carbs, 6 g fiber, 12 g protein

Ingredients:
- old fashioned oatmeal (3 cups, cooked)
- quinoa (3 cups, cooked)
- 4 cups banana, peeled, chopped

Directions:
1. Combine the oatmeal and quinoa and mix well. Evenly divide into four bowls and top with the bananas before serving.

Sweet Potato Hash with Sausage & Spinach

Yields: 4   Prep: 5 mins.   Cook: 15 mins.

Nutrition per Serving:

544 calories, 2 g fat, 65 g carbs, 2 g fiber, 11 g protein

Ingredients:

- sweet potatoes (4 small, chopped)
- apples (2, cored and chopped)
- 1 clove garlic (minced)
- sausage (1 lb., ground)
- spinach (10 oz chopped)
- Salt & pepper

Directions:

1. Brown the sausage until no pink remains. Add the remaining ingredients.
2. Cook for an additional 5-6 minutes, or until the spinach and apples are tender. Season to taste and serve hot.

Cajun Omelet

Yields: 2   Prep: 5 mins.   Cook: 8 mins.

Nutrition per Serving:

467 calories, 14 g fat, 11 g carbs, 2 g fiber, 3 g protein

Ingredients:

- sausage (1/4 lb., spicy)
- mushrooms (1/3 cup, sliced)
- onion (1/2, diced eggs (4 large)
- ½ medium bell pepper, chopped
- water (2 tbsp.)
- cooking Fat
- 1 pinch cayenne pepper (optional)
- Sea salt & fresh pepper to taste

Directions:

1. Brown the sausage in a medium saucepan until cooked through. Add the mushrooms, onion and bell pepper and cook for another 3-5 minutes, or until tender.
2. Meanwhile, whisk together the eggs, water, mustard and spices. Season with the salt and pepper.
3. Top with your eggs over then reduce to a low heat. Cook until the top is nearly set and then fold the omelet in half and cover. Cook for another minute before serving hot.

Strawberry Cashew Chia Pudding

Yields: 2   Prep: 10 mins.   Cook: 0 mins.
Nutrition per Serving:
223 calories, 12 g fat, 18 g carbs, 2 g fiber, 10 g protein

Ingredients:
- ❖ chia seeds (6 tbsp.)
- ❖ cashew milk (2 cups, unsweetened)
- ❖ Strawberries, for topping

Directions:
1. Combine the chia seeds and milk and mix well. Refrigerate overnight. Stir in the berries and serve.

Peanut Butter Banana Oatmeal

Yields: 1   Prep: 5 mins.   Cook: 5 mins.
Nutrition per Serving:
645 calories, 32g fat, 65 g carbs, 5 g fiber, 26g protein

Ingredients:
- ❖ quick oats (1/3 cup)
- ❖ cinnamon (1/4 tsp. (optional)
- ❖ banana (1/2, sliced)
- ❖ peanut butter (1 tbsp., unsweetened)

Directions:
1. Combine all ingredients in a bowl with a lid. Refrigerate.

Overnight Peach Oatmeal

Yields: 2   Prep: 10 mins.   Cook: 0 mins.

Nutrition per Serving:

282 calories, 6 g fat, 48 g carbs, 2 g fiber, 10 g protein

Ingredients:
- oats (½ cup, old fashioned)
- skim milk (2/3 cup)
- Greek yogurt (½ cup, plain)
- chia seeds   (1 tbsp.)
- vanilla (½ tsp.)
- peach (½ cup, peeled, diced)
- banana (1 medium, peeled, chopped)

Directions:
1. Combine the oats, milk, yogurt, chia seeds and vanilla in a bowl with a lid.
2. Refrigerate for 12 hours.
3. Top with fruit before serving.

Mediterranean Salmon and Potato Salad

Yields: 4   Prep: 15 mins.   Cook: 18 mins.
Nutrition per Serving:
463 calories, 4 g fat, 75 g carbs, 18 g fiber, 34g protein

Ingredients:

- ❖ red potatoes (1 lb., peeled, cut into wedges)
- ❖ extra virgin olive oil (1/2 cup, plus 2 tbs more)
- ❖ balsamic vinegar (2 tbs)
- ❖ fresh rosemary (1 tbs, minced)
- ❖ peas (2 cups, cooked, drained)
- ❖ salmon fillets (4, 4 oz each)
- ❖ lemon juice (2 tbs)
- ❖ salt (1/4 tsp)
- ❖ English cucumbers (2 cups, sliced, seedless)

Directions:

1. In a medium saucepan, bring water to a boil and cook potatoes until tender, about 10 minutes.
2. Drain and pour potatoes back into pan. To make dressing, in a small bowl, whisk together 1/2 cup of olive oil, vinegar and rosemary.
3. Combine potatoes and peas with dressing. Set aside. In a separate medium pan, heat the remaining 2 tbs of olive oil over medium heat.
4. Add salmon fillets and sprinkle with lemon juice and salt.
5. Cook for 4 minutes on both side or until fish flakes easily. To serve, place cucumber slices on a serving platter top with potato salad and fish fillets.

Celery Soup

Yields: 4   Prep: 8 mins.   Cook: 10 mins.
Nutrition per Serving:
51 calories, 3 g fat, 4 g carbs, 2 g fiber, 2 g protein

Ingredients:
- ❖ olive oil (1 tbs)
- ❖ garlic cloves (3, minced)
- ❖ celery (2 lbs., fresh, chopped into
- ❖ one-inch pieces.)
- ❖ vegetable stock (6 cups)
- ❖ salt (1 tsp)

Directions:
1. Reserve celery tops for later use. Heat up the oil over medium heat in a soup pot.
2. Cook garlic until softened, about 3-5 minutes. Add celery stalks, salt and vegetable stock and bring to a boil.
3. Cover and reduce heat to low and simmer until celery softens. Let the soup cool for a bit then and puree with a hand blender.
4. Add and cook the celery tops on medium heat for 5 minutes.

Pea Tuna Salad

Yields: 4   Prep: 1 hr. 15 mins. Cook: 10 mins.
Nutrition per Serving:
246 calories, 13 g fat, 11 g carbs, 1 g fiber, 22 g protein

Ingredients:
- Peas (3 lbs., cooked)
- mayonnaise (1/2 cup, low fat)
- tarragon vinegar (1/3 cup)
- honey Dijon mustard (1 tsp)
- shallots (2 small, sliced thinly)
- tuna fish (2 (6 oz) cans, drained)
- sprigs fresh tarragon (2 small, chopped finel

Directions:
1. In a large bowl, combine mayonnaise, vinegar and mustard. Add tuna fish, shallots and peas; toss to coat with dressing.
2. Cover and refrigerate one hour prior to serving. Garnish with fresh tarragon and serve.

Vegetable Soup

Yields: 4   Prep: 15 mins.   Cook: 1 hr. 5 mins.

Nutrition per Serving:
242 calories, 8 g fat, 34 g carbs, 13 g fiber, 12 g protein

Ingredients:

- extra virgin olive oil (2 tbsp)
- garlic cloves (4, chopped finely)
- celery stalks (2, sliced finely)
- carrots (2, sliced finely)
- water (6 cups or chicken broth)
- thyme (1/4 tsp)
- rosemary (1/4 tsp)
- bay leaf (1)
- Peas (1 can (14 oz)
- salt (1/2 tsp)

Directions:

1. Heat up the oil over medium heat in a soup pot. Add garlic, celery, and carrots and continue to cook for 5 minutes, stirring occasionally.
2. Add water or chicken broth, thyme, rosemary and bay leaf and cook until it comes to a boil.
3. Reduce heat and cover and simmer gently for about 45-60 minutes. Add peas and season with salt.
4. Let soup cool slightly, remove bay leaf and puree with a hand blender, until creamy. Serve in warmed soup bowls.

Carrot & Turkey Soup

Yields: 4   Prep: 15 mins.   Cook: 40 mins.
Nutrition per Serving:
436 calories, 12 g fat, 20 g carbs, 6 g fiber, 59 g protein

Ingredients:
- Ground turkey (1/2 lb, lean)
- frozen carrot (1/2 bag)
- green peas (1/4 cup)
- chicken broth (1 can (32 oz)
- tomatoes (2 medium, seeded, and roughly chopped)
- garlic powder (1 tsp)
- paprika (1 tsp)
- oregano (1 tsp)
- bay leaf (1)

Directions:
1. Over medium heat, brown the ground turkey in a soup pot. Add peas, frozen carrot, paprika, tomatoes, garlic powder, bay leaf, oregano, and broth.
2. Bring pot to a boil, reduce heat, cover, and simmer for 30 minutes.

Creamy Pumpkin Soup

Yields: 4-6   Prep: 15 mins.   Cook: 1 hr. 10 mins.

Nutrition per Serving:

332 calories, 18 g fat, 32 g carbs, 9 g fiber, 12g protein

Ingredients:

- ❖ pumpkin (1, cut lengthwise, seeds removed, peeled)
- ❖ sweet potato (1, cut lengthwise, peeled)
- ❖ olive oil (2 tbs)
- ❖ garlic cloves (4, unpeeled)
- ❖ vegetable stock (4 cups)
- ❖ light cream (1/4 cup)
- ❖ Salt

Directions:

1. Preheat oven to 375 degrees. Cut all the side of the pumpkin, shallots and sweet potato with oil.
2. Transfer your vegetables with your garlic onto a roasting pan. Set to roast for about 40 minutes or until tender.
3. Let the vegetables cool for a time and scoop out flesh of the sweet potato and pumpkin.
4. In a soup pot, place flesh of roasted vegetables, shallots and peeled garlic. Add broth and bring to a boil.
5. Reduce heat, and let it simmer, covered for 30 minutes, stir occasionally. Let the soup cool.
6. Puree soup with a hand blender, until smooth. Add cream.
7. Season to taste and simmer until warmed through, about 5 minutes. Serve in warm soup bowls.

Chicken Pea Soup

Yields: 4-6   Prep: 15 mins.   Cook: 55 mins.
Nutrition per Serving:
176 calories, 5 g fat, 18 g carbs, 6 g fiber, 15 g protein

Ingredients:

- ❖ chicken breast (1 lb. skinless, boneless, cubed)
- ❖ olive oil (2 tbs)
- ❖ garlic cloves (3, minced)
- ❖ carrots (3, grated)
- ❖ bay leaf (1)
- ❖ salt (1 tsp)
- ❖ poultry seasoning (1 tsp)
- ❖ chicken broth (8 cups)
- ❖ dried split peas (1/2 cup, washed and drained)
- ❖ green peas (1 cup)

Directions:

1. Heat up the olive oil over medium heat in a soup pot. Add chicken and cook for 5 minutes, until lightly browned.
2. Add garlic, bay leaf, carrots, salt and seasoning and cook until vegetables soften, stirring occasionally.
3. Add broth and split peas to pot and bring to a boil. Reduce heat, cover and simmer on low heat for 30-45 minutes.
4. Add green peas to the soup and heat for 5 minutes, stirring to combine all ingredients.

Shrimp & Pasta Salad

Yields: 2   Prep: 15 mins.   Cook: 12 mins.
Nutrition per Serving:
516 calories, 20 g fat, 55 g carbs, 7 g fiber, 32 g protein

Ingredients:

- ❖ White refined pasta (1/2 lb., shells or tubes)
- ❖ shrimp (3/4 lb. medium, peeled, deveined, and cooked)
- ❖ fresh spinach (2 cups)
- ❖ Roma tomatoes (2 medium, seeded and chopped)
- ❖ light ranch salad dressing (1/2 cup)
- ❖ basil (4 tbs, chopped coarsely)
- ❖ parmesan cheese (1/4 cup, grated)

Directions:

1. Bring a salted water to boil in a pot. Cook the pasta as the package instructed. Drain the water from the pasta.
2. In a bowl, combine cooked pasta, spinach, salad dressing, tomatoes and shrimp. Refrigerate for 20 minutes.
3. Toss together with basil and cheese. Serve.

Homemade Rice Salad

Yields: 6   Prep: 15 mins.   Cook: 8 mins.
Nutrition per Serving:
425 calories, 6 g fat, 84 g carbs, 6 g fiber, 9 g protein

Ingredients:

- ❖ olive oil (1 1/2 tbs)
- ❖ green bell peppers (2 medium, seeded, chopped, cooked)
- ❖ carrots (2 medium, diced, cooked)
- ❖ mushrooms (1 cup, sliced, cooked)
- ❖ potatoes (2 medium, peeled, cooked, cubed)
- ❖ cumin (1/2 tsp)
- ❖ oregano (1/2 tsp)
- ❖ soy sauce (1 ½ tbs, low sodium)
- ❖ instant white rice (3 cups, cooked, cooled)
- ❖ fresh Italian parsley (1/4 cup, chopped)
- ❖ lemon juice (2 tbs)

Directions:
1. Heat the olive oil up over medium heat. Cook peppers, green beans, and carrots for about 5 minutes.
2. Add mushrooms and potatoes and continue cooking 2 - 3 minutes. Add cumin, oregano and soy sauce.
3. Transfer mixture to a large salad bowl and allow to cool to room temperature.
4. Add rice, chopped parsley and lemon juice. Mix together until combined. Serve.

Haddock Noodle Soup

Yields: 2   Prep: 15 mins.   Cook: 10 mins.

Nutrition per Serving:

509 calories, 6 g fat, 80 g carbs, 4 g fiber, 33 g protein

Ingredients:

For the Fish Balls:

- ❖ whole haddock fillets (7- ounces, skinned, and finely chopped)
- ❖ squid (2- ounces, cleaned)
- ❖ Pinch of sea salt flakes
- ❖ pinch of ground white pepper
- ❖ rice wine (1 teaspoon)
- ❖ cornstarch (1 tablespoon)
- ❖ egg white (1 large)
- ❖ oyster sauce (1 teaspoon)
- ❖ cilantro stems (1 tablespoon finely sliced)

For the Broth:

- ❖ fresh fish stock (1 1/2 quarts)
- ❖ vermicelli noodles (7- ounces cooked, refined white)
- ❖ pinch of sea salt flakes
- ❖ pinch of ground white pepper
- ❖ low-sodium light soy sauce (1 tablespoon)
- ❖ toasted sesame oil (1 teaspoon)

To Serve:

- ❖ chili oil (1 teaspoon, or to taste)
- ❖ Cilantro leave
- ❖ chives (1 tablespoon, finely chopped)

Directions:

1. Put the squid and haddock into a food processor, season with the white pepper, salt, rice wine, oyster sauce, cornstarch and egg white, and blend until it is airy and light.
2. Sprinkle the cilantro stems and mix well. Use 2 tablespoons, to create an oval ball out of the fish mixture.
3. You should get 12 balls out of it. Add the fish stock in a wok and bring to a simmer.
4. Add the already cooked noodles and add white pepper and sea salt. Turn the heat to medium, and gently add the fish balls to the wok.
5. Cook for 3 minutes or until the fish balls float to the surface and turn opaque white. Season with the sesame oil and light soy sauce.
6. Have the noodles divide between two bowls, ladle in the stock and place six fish balls into each bowl.
7. Drizzle with the chili oil, sprinkle over the cilantro leave and chives, and serve immediately.

Baked Chicken Breasts

Yields: 4   Prep: 5 mins.   Cook: 15 mins.

Nutrition per Serving:

205 calories, 10 g fat, 1 g carbs, 3 g fiber, 27 g protein

Ingredients:
- ❖ 4 boneless, skinless chicken breasts
- ❖ 2 tbsp. Extra Virgin Olive Oil
- ❖ 1 tsp. kosher salt
- ❖ 1/2 tsp. black pepper 1/2 tsp garlic powder
- ❖ 1/2 tsp. onion powder
- ❖ 1/2 tsp. chili powder

Directions:
1. Turn your oven on and allow to preheat up to 450 degrees F. Lightly grease a 9x13-inch baking dish.
2. Pound the chicken breasts until they are an even ¾-inch thick. Lightly coat the chicken with olive oil.
3. Whisk together the salt, pepper, garlic powder, onion powder and chili powder.
4. Season the chicken on both sides with the spice mixture and place in the prepared pan.
5. Set to bake in the preheated oven for about 20 minutes (checking after the 15-minute mark), or until the chicken is cooked through.
6. Rest for 5-10 minutes, covered with foil, then slice and serve.

Dump Pot Chicken & Rice

Yields: 4   Prep: 10 mins.   Cook: 25 mins.
Nutrition per Serving:
177 calories, 1 g fat, 31 g carbs, 1 g fiber, 11 g protein

Ingredients:
- ❖ chicken white meat (1 lb., strips)
- ❖ 2 cups cooked basmati rice
- ❖ water (1/4 cup)
- ❖ soy sauce (1/4 cup, low sodium)
- ❖ lemon juice (1/2 cup))
- ❖ extra-virgin olive oil (3 tbsp.)
- ❖ ½ tsp salt
- ❖ ¼ tsp ground pepper
- ❖ 2 tbsp. chives, finely chopped

Directions:
1. Combine the water, soy sauce and lemon in a small bowl. Mix well.
2. Heat 2 Tbs olive oil and cook the chicken over medium high heat in a skillet until cooked through.
3. Add the soy mixture. Simmer for 15 minutes to reduce the sauce. Add in the remaining ingredients, except chives, and season to taste.
4. Continue to cook for 4-5 minutes, or until the rice is heated through. Garnish with chives and serve.

Italian Inspired Chicken Skillet

Yields: 4   Prep: 10 mins.   Cook: 20 mins.
Nutrition per Serving:
278 calories, 11 g fat, 12 g carbs, 8 g fiber, 34 g protein

Ingredients:

- chicken breasts (4 large, boneless skinless cut 1/4-inch thin)
- dried oregano (1 tbsp., divided)
- salt (1 tsp)
- black pepper (1 tsp., divided)
- olive oil (3 tbsp.)
- baby Bella mushrooms (8 oz., cleaned, trimmed, and sliced)
- grape tomatoes (14 oz., halved)
- garlic (2 tbsp., fresh, chopped)
- chicken or vegetable stock (1/2 cup)
- lemon juice (1 tbsp., freshly squeezed)
- chicken broth (3/4 cup)
- Handful baby spinach (optional)

Directions:

1. Season the chicken on both sides with half of the oregano, salt and pepper.
2. Heat 2 Tbs of oil in a heavy skillet and brown the chicken on both sides for 3 minutes.
3. Remove the chicken and set aside. Sauté the mushrooms in the same skillet, add another tablespoon of oil if needed.
4. Add the tomatoes, garlic and remaining oregano, salt and pepper.
5. Cook for another 3 minutes. Deglaze the pan with the chicken or vegetable stock and then stir in the chicken broth and lemon juice.
6. Bring the liquid to a boil and then return the chicken to the pan.
7. Reduce heat to medium and simmer for 8-10 minutes, or until the chicken is fully cooked and the liquid is reduced to desired consistency.
8. Serve with rice or quinoa, if desired.

Turkey Burgers with Cucumber Salad

Yields: 4   Prep: 15 mins.   Cook: 15 mins.

Nutrition per Serving:

314 calories, 0 g fat, 15 g carbs, 3 g fiber, 26 g protein

Ingredients:

Turkey burgers:
- ❖ turkey (1 lb., lean ground)
- ❖ egg (1 large, beaten)
- ❖ oatmeal (½ cup)
- ❖ onions (1/3 cup, grated)
- ❖ parsley (1/3 cup, finely chopped)
- ❖ garlic (1 clove, minced)
- ❖ sea salt (½ tsp)
- ❖ black pepper (½ tsp)

- ❖ olive oil (1 tbsp., extra-virgin)
- ❖ canola oil (2 tsp.)

Cucumber salad:
- ❖ cucumber (1, diced small)
- ❖ chives (1/2 cup, chopped)
- ❖ ripe tomato (1 medium, finely diced)
- ❖ freshly squeezed lime or lemon juice (2 tbsp.)
- ❖ ¼ tsp kosher or sea salt

Directions:

1. Combine the turkey burger ingredients, except oil, and mix well. Form into 4 patties.
2. Lightly grease the grill and grill the patties for 5-6 minutes per side on medium high.
3. Meanwhile, combine the cucumber salad ingredients and chill until serving.

Saltfish Salad

Yields: 4   Prep: 30 mins.   Cook: 0 mins.
Nutrition per Serving:
613 calories, 28 g fat, 9 g carbs, 4 g fiber, 78 g protein

Ingredients:

- salted cod (1 lb.)
- yellow onion (1 large, thinly sliced)
- tomato (1 large, diced)
- eggs (3 hard-boiled, quartered)
- green olives (12, optional)
- olive oil (1/4 cup)
- chicken or vegetable stock (1 tbsp.)

Directions:

1. Soak the cod in cold water for 15-30 minutes. Drain and place in a large pot. Cover the cod with water and bring to a boil.
2. Change the water and bring to a simmer another 3-4 times, or until the cod is reduced to the appropriate saltiness.
3. Drain and break the cod into pieces. Sauté the onion with olive oil for 5-6 minutes, or until soft.
4. Add all your ingredients to a bowl then mix until it is fully combined. Serve with rice and drizzled with olive oil.

Taco Salad

Yields: 6   Prep: 15 mins.   Cook: 10 mins.
Nutrition per Serving:
196 calories, 0 g fat, 9 g carbs, 2 g fiber, 15 g protein

Ingredients:
Salad:
- ground turkey (1/2 lb.)
- chili powder (1 tsp.)
- cumin (1/2 tsp.)
- garlic powder (1/4 tsp.)
- sea salt (1/4 tsp.)
- cheddar cheese, reduced fat (1/2 cup, shredded)

- romaine lettuce (3 cups, chopped)
- cherry tomatoes (1 cup, halved)
- salsa (1/2 cup)

Creamy Salsa Dressing (optional):
- Greek yogurt (2 tbsp., plain)
- Juice of 1 lime
- salsa (1/4 cup)

Directions:
1. Brown the turkey in a skillet over medium high heat until cooked through. Add the spices and mix well.
2. Allow the meat to cool before layering the salad. Place the salsa in the bottom of a jar or bow and top with the turkey, tomatoes, lettuce and cheese.
3. Combine the dressing ingredients in a blender or bowl and mix well. Drizzle on the dressing before serving.

Baked Sweet Potatoes

Yields: 6-8   Prep: 15 mins.   Cook: 25 mins.
Nutrition per Serving:
790 calories, 1 g fat, 20 g carbs, 6 g fiber, 4 g protein

Ingredients:

- ❖ sweet potatoes (4 pounds, peeled and cut to large bite-sized pieces)
- ❖ orange juice (2 cups)
- ❖ light corn syrup (3 cups)
- ❖ ground cinnamon (1 tsp)
- ❖ ground nutmeg (1 tsp)
- ❖ vanilla extract (¼ cup)
- ❖ lemon zest (2 tsp)
- ❖ flour (2 tbs, refined white)
- ❖ light brown sugar (1 ½ cups, packed)
- ❖ granulated sugar (1 ½ cups)

Directions:

1. Preheat oven to 350 degrees. Boil sweet potatoes until slightly underdone.
2. Drain, cool and set aside. In a large bowl, whisk together the zest, vanilla, cinnamon, nutmeg, corn syrup and orange juice.
3. In another bowl, combine sugars and both flour together. Add in your sweet potatoes to a baking dish. Top with your dry ingredient mixture then stir until coated. Pour the liquid over yams and bake for about 25 minutes.
4. Serve and enjoy!

Italian Styled Stuffed Zucchini Boats

Yields: 6   Prep: 5 mins.   Cook: 25 mins.

Nutrition per Serving:

298 calories, 17 g fat, 14 g carbs, 2 g fiber, 25 g protein

Ingredients:

- ❖ zucchini (6 large)
- ❖ olive oil
- ❖ kosher salt
- ❖ freshly ground black pepper
- ❖ garlic powder (1/4 tsp.)
- ❖ yellow onion (1 small, diced)
- ❖ garlic (2 cloves, minced)
- ❖ ground turkey (1 lb.)
- ❖ crush tomatoes (1 (28 oz.) can)
- ❖ mozzarella cheese (4 oz., shredded)
- ❖ parmesan cheese (1 oz., freshly grated)
- ❖ flat leaf parsley for garnish

Directions:

1. Turn your oven on and allow to preheat up to 425 degrees F and lightly grease a 9x13-inch baking dish with cooking spray.
2. Slice the zucchini in half lengthwise and then scoop out the seeds. Brush with olive oil and season with salt, pepper and garlic powder.
3. Roast in the prepared dish for 20 minutes, or until it begins to soften.
4. Meanwhile, sauté the onions and garlic in a ½ tbsp of olive oil over medium high heat in a large skillet.
5. Cook for 3-4 minutes, then add the ground turkey and brown. Add the tomatoes and bring to a boil.
6. Reduce heat to medium and then let simmer until the zucchini are done. Stir in ½ tsp salt and pepper to taste.
7. Fill the zucchini boats with the meat mixture and sprinkle on shredded cheese.
8. Set to bake for about 5 minutes or at least until the cheese you added has melted, about 3-5 minutes.
9. Serve hot, garnished with parmesan cheese and parsley.

Chicken Cutlets

Yields: 4   Prep: 15 mins.   Cook: 15 mins.

Nutrition per Serving:

549 calories, 6 g fat, 7g carbs, 1 g fiber, 114g protein

Ingredients:

- red wine vinegar (4 tsp)
- minced garlic (2 tsp)
- dried sage leaves (2 tsp)
- chicken breast cutlets (1 pound)
- Salt and pepper, to taste
- flour (1/4 cup, refined white)
- olive oil (2 tsp)
- reduced-sodium fat-free chicken broth (1/2 cup)
- lemon juice (1 tbs)

Directions:

1. Lay a good amount of plastic wrap on the kitchen counter; sprinkle with half the combine sage, garlic and vinegar.
2. Put the chicken breast on the plastic wrap; sprinkle with the rest of the vinegar mixture. Season lightly with pepper and salt.
3. Cover the chicken with a second sheet of plastic wrap. Use a kitchen mallet to pound the breast until it is flattened. Let stand 5 minutes.
4. Coat the chicken on both sides with flour. In a skillet, heat up the oil over medium heat.
5. Add half of the chicken breast and cook for 1 ½ minutes or until it is browned on bottom.
6. Turn on the other side and let it cook for 3 minutes.
7. Remove the chicken breast and place it on a to oven-proof serving platter so that you can keep warm.
8. Do the same step with the rest of the cutlets. Heat up the lemon juice and the broth to a boil in skillet.
9. Reduce the liquid by half. Pour mixture over the chicken breast; serve immediately.

Slow Cooker Salsa Turkey

Yields: 8   Prep: 5 mins.   Cook: 8 hrs.

Nutrition per Serving:

178 calories, 4 g fat, 7 g carbs, 2 g fiber, 27 g protein

Ingredients:

- ❖ turkey breasts (2 pounds, boneless and skinless)
- ❖ salsa (1 cup)
- ❖ tomatoes (1 cup, petite, diced, canned choose low sodium)
- ❖ Taco Seasoning (2 tablespoons)
- ❖ Celery (1/2 cup, diced fine)
- ❖ Carrots (1/2 cup, shredded)
- ❖ sour cream (3 tablespoons, reduced fat)

Directions:

1. Add your turkey to your slow cooker. Season your turkey with taco seasoning then top with your salsa and vegetables.
2. Add in ½ cup of water. Set to cook on low 7 hours (internal temperature should be 165°F when done).
3. Shred the turkey with 2 forks, add in sour cream and stir. Enjoy.

Sriracha Lime Chicken & Apple Salad

Yields: 4   Prep: 10 mins.   Cook: 15 mins.

Nutrition per Serving:

484 calories, 28 g fat, 32g carbs, 8 g fiber, 30 g protein

Ingredients:

Sriracha Lime Chicken:
- chicken breasts (2 organic)
- sriracha (3 tbsp.)
- lime (1, juiced)
- fine sea salt (1/4 tsp.)
- freshly ground pepper (1/4 tsp.)

Fruit Salad:
- apple (4, peeled, cored, diced)
- grape tomatoes (1 cup organic)
- red onion (1/3 cup, finely chopped)

Lime Vinaigrette:
- light olive oil (1/3 cup)
- apple cider vinegar (1/4 cup)
- limes (2, juiced)
- dash fine sea salt

Directions:

1. Use your salt and pepper to season the chicken on both sides. Spread on the sriracha and lime and let the chicken sit for 20 minutes.
2. Cook the chicken for 3-4 minutes per side over medium heat, or until done. Grill the apple with the chicken.
3. Meanwhile, whisk together the dressing and season to taste. Dress the salad and serve as a side to the chicken and apple.

Garlic Parmesan Chicken & Potatoes

Yields: 2   Prep: 10 mins.   Cook: 40 mins.

Nutrition per Serving:

382 calories, 23 g fat, 24 g carbs, 6 g fiber, 10 g protein

Ingredients:

- chicken thighs (6 bone-in, skin-on)
- Italian seasoning (1 tbsp.)
- Salt (kosher) and grounded black pepper, to taste
- butter (3 tbsp., unsalted, divided)
- baby spinach (3 cups, roughly chopped)
- baby Dutch potatoes (16 oz., halved)
- fresh parsley leaves (2 tbsp., chopped)

- For the garlic parmesan cream sauce
- butter (1/4 cup, unsalted)
- garlic (4 cloves, minced)
- cream cheese (2 tbsp.)
- chicken broth (1/2 cup)
- dried thyme (1 tbsp.)
- dried basil (1/2 tsp.)
- half and half (1/2 cup)
- Parmesan (1/2 cup, freshly grated)
- Salt (kosher) & grounded black pepper, to taste

Directions:

1. Turn your oven on and allow to preheat up to 400 degrees F and lightly grease a 9x13-inch baking dish.
2. Season the chicken with Italian seasoning, salt and pepper. Sear the chicken for 2-3 minutes per side in 2 tbsp. of butter in a large skillet.
3. Remove and set aside. Add the remaining butter into the skillet and cook the spinach for 2 minutes, or until wilted.
4. Melt the butter in a skillet and sauté the garlic for 1-2 minutes. Melt the cream cheese and then stir in the chicken broth, thyme and basil.
5. Cook for 1-2 minutes. Stir in the half and half and cheese until thickened, about 2 minutes. Season to taste with salt and pepper.
6. Place the chicken in the baking dish and top with the potatoes, spinach and then pour the cream sauce over the top. Bake for 25-30 minutes, or until cooked through. Garnish with parsley before serving.

Turkey & Vegetable Quesadillas

Yields: 4   Prep: 10 mins.   Cook: 10 mins.

Nutrition per Serving:

243 calories, 9 g fat, 15 g carbs, 2 g fiber, 26 g protein

Ingredients:

- Greek yogurt (1/4 cup, low-fat, plain)
- Turkey breast (12 ounces boneless and skinless)
- Ranch Seasoning Blend (2 tsp)
- canola oil (1 tsp)
- orange bell peppers (2, top and bottom removed, cored and seeded)
- tortillas (4, refined white)
- tomatoes (2, diced, seedless)
- pepper Jack cheese (1/2 cup shredded)

Directions:

1. Create a sauce by combining a half of a teaspoon of your seasoning blend with your yogurt. Cover and set to chill.
2. Transfer your turkey to a plastic bag then pound with a meat mallet to 1/4-inch thickness. Add in your remaining seasoning and oil.
3. Leave your meat to marinate for at least 10 mins. Set a skillet on moderate heat to get hot then add in your peppers.
4. Press your peppers down for about 2 minutes to sear. Cool and dice.
5. Add your turkey into your skillet and toss the marinade. Cook over medium heat for 5 minutes.
6. Flip, and continue to cook until done (should be at 165° F). Transfer to a plate, cool and dice. Clean the skillet using paper towels.
7. Replace on medium heat. Place a tortilla in your skillet, top with half of the peppers, cheese, tomatoes, and peppers.
8. Cover with a second tortilla then cook for another 2 minutes per side. Transfer to a cutting board. Use a pizza cutter to slice in half then serve.

Roasted Salmon

Yields: 4   Prep: 5 mins.   Cook: 20 mins.
Nutrition per Serving:
222 calories, 1 g fat, 4 g carbs, 1 g fiber, 26 g protein

Ingredients:

- Salmon (1 whole, 2 ½ - pounds, cleaned and scaled)
- Garlic-Infused (3 tablespoons)
- Kosher salt
- Freshly ground black pepper
- fresh flat leaf parsley (¼ cup (8 g) chopped)
- fresh herb of your choice (¼ cup, chopped)
- scallions (¼ cup chopped, green parts only)
- lemon (1, thinly sliced crosswise)

Directions:

1. Position rack in upper third of oven. Preheat the oven to 450°F. Prepare a rimmed roasted pan for your fish.
2. Allow to stand at room temperature while your oven preheats.
3. Place fish on pan and make 3 crosswise slashes, all the way down to the bone, on each side of the fish.
4. Use your garlic oil to rub your inside and out then season to your liking. Toss your scallions and herbs together.
5. Press some of your herbs and a lemon slice on each serving then use the remainder to stuff the fish cavity.
6. Set to roast until done (about 20 mins). Enjoy!

Chicken & Veggie Quesadillas

Yields: 4   Prep: 10 mins.   Cook: 10 mins.
Nutrition per Serving:
243 calories, 9 g fat, 15 g carbs, 2 g fiber, 26 g protein

Ingredients:

- Greek yogurt (1/4 cup, low-fat, plain)
- Chicken breast (12 ounces boneless and skinless)
- Ranch Seasoning Blend (2 tsp)
- canola oil (1 tsp)
- orange bell peppers (2, top and
- bottom removed, cored, and seeded)
- tortillas (4, refined white)
- tomatoes (2, diced, seedless)
- pepper Jack cheese (1/2 cup shredded)

Directions:

1. Create a sauce by combining a half of a teaspoon of your seasoning blend with your yogurt. Cover and set to chill.
2. Transfer your chicken to a plastic bag then pound with a meat mallet to 1/4-inch thickness. Add in your remaining seasoning and oil.
3. Leave your meat to marinate for at least 10 mins. Set a skillet on moderate heat to get hot then add in your peppers.
4. Press your peppers down for about 2 minutes to sear. Cool and dice.
5. Add your chicken into your skillet and toss the marinade. Cook over medium heat for 5 minutes.
6. Flip, and continue to cook until done (should be at 165° F). Transfer to a plate, cool and dice. Clean the skillet using paper towels.
7. Replace on medium heat. Place a tortilla in your skillet, top with half of the peppers, cheese, tomatoes, and peppers.
8. Cover with a second tortilla then cook for another 2 minutes per side. Transfer to a cutting board.
9. Use a pizza cutter to slice in half then serve.

Fajita Stuffed Chicken

Yields: 2   Prep: 15 mins.   Cook: 30 mins.
Nutrition per Serving:
591 calories, 18 g fat, 45 g carbs, 4 g fiber, 60 g protein

Ingredients:

- chicken breasts (4)
- olive oil (2 tbsp.)
- taco seasoning (2 tbsp.)
- ½ each red, yellow and green pepper, diced
- red onion (1 small, diced)
- shredded cheese (1/2 cup, shredded)
- Cilantro (optional for garnish)
- Salsa and sour cream

- Roasted sweet potatoes (optional side)
- olive oil (1 tbsp.)
- sweet potatoes (3, cut into 1-inch pieces)
- chili powder (2 tsp.)
- paprika (2 tsp.)
- garlic powder (2 tsp.)
- salt (1 tsp.)

Directions:

1. Turn your oven on and allow to preheat up to 450 degrees F.
2. Coat the sweet potatoes in olive oil and the spices and roast in a baking dish or sheet pan for 25-30 minutes, or until tender.
3. Meanwhile, make a slit in the side of each chicken breast. Combine the bell peppers and onions and stuff into the slit.
4. Grill the chicken for 15 minutes on medium high. Sprinkle on the cheese and grill for another 5 minutes, or until the cheese is melted.
5. Serve with the sweet potatoes and other toppings of choice.

Chicken Chili with Winter Squash

Yields: 8   Prep: 15 mins.   Cook: 45 mins.
Nutrition per Serving:
298 calories, 1 g fat, 28 g carbs, 2 g fiber, 34 g protein

Ingredients:

- Garlic-Infused oil (3 tablespoons)
- ground chicken (2- pounds)
- leeks (3/4 cup finely chopped, green parts only)
- scallions (1/4 cup (16, finely chopped, green parts only)
- green bell pepper (1, cored, finely chopped)
- red bell pepper (1, cored, finely chopped)
- cumin (1 tablespoons)
- paprika (1 teaspoon)
- smoked paprika (1 teaspoon)
- chile powder (¼ to ½ teaspoon)
- dried oregano (1/2 teaspoon)
- kosher salt (1/2 teaspoon)
- freshly ground black pepper (¼ teaspoon)
- Chicken Stock (2 cups)
- Tomatoes (2 (14.5 ounces) cans diced, drained well)
- Tomato Sauce (1, 15-ounce)
- butternut squash (10 ½ ounces, peeled, cut into large bite-sized chunks)
- black beans (7- ounces, drained, canned)
- fine ground yellow cornmeal (1/4 cup)

Directions:
1. Heat 1 tablespoon of oil in a heavy bottomed large Dutch oven over low-medium heat and add the ground chicken, breaking it up with a spatula.
2. Sauté until the chicken loses all of its pink color. Remove from pan and set aside.
3. Add in the rest of your oil on low-medium heat. Once hot, add in your scallions and leeks then until tender (about 2 minutes). Add in the chopped peppers and sauté until crisp-tender.
4. Stir in the spices, salt and pepper, using smaller amount of hot chili.
5. Sauté for about 15 seconds, then add the reserved chicken. Stir in your tomatoes, tomato sauce, squash and stock.
6. Cover adjust heat and cook for about 20 to 30 minutes or until squash is tender. Taste and adjust seasoning as desired.
7. Combine your cornmeal with a ladle of the chili liquid to make a paste.
8. Stir your cornmeal paste into the chili and distribute well. Cover then allow to simmer for about another 5 minutes to thicken. Serve hot

Grilled Lemon Rosemary Chicken

Yields: 8   Prep: 10 mins.   Cook: 0 mins.
Nutrition per Serving:
251 calories, 11 g fat, 1 g carbs, 3 g fiber, 35 g protein

Ingredients:
- ❖ chicken breast fillets (2 lbs.)
- ❖ olive oil (1/4 cup)
- ❖ garlic (3 cloves, minced)
- ❖ zest from one lemon

- ❖ juice from one lemon (about ¼ cup)
- ❖ salt (3/4 tsp.)
- ❖ pepper (1/4 tsp.)
- ❖ rosemary (1 large sprig)

Directions:
1. Combine all ingredients in a bag and mix well. Refrigerate for 3 hours to allow the chicken to marinate.
2. Grill over medium heat for 3-4 minutes per side, or until cooked through. Serve hot.

Spaghetti Squash in Tomato Sauce

Yields: 2   Prep: 10 mins.   Cook: 1hr.
Nutrition per Serving:
113 calories, 8 g fat, 12g carbs, 2 g fiber, 2 g protein

Ingredients:
- ❖ Spaghetti Squash (1 cup)
- ❖ Olive Oil (1 tbs)

- ❖ Seasonings, to taste
- ❖ tomato sauce (1 cup)

Directions:
1. Cut spaghetti squash in half and drizzle with olive oil. Sprinkle on desired seasonings and bake cut-side-down at 400 degrees for about an hour.
2. The squash should be very tender when finished. Allow squash to cool for a few minutes, then take a fork and scrape out the squash "noodles".
3. Serve and cover with lemon juice, olive oil, and garlic or the spaghetti sauce of your choosing.

Jalapeño Turkey Burgers

Yields: 4   Prep: 10 mins.   Cook: 10 mins.
Nutrition per Serving:
248 calories, 9 g fat, 19 g carbs, 1 g fiber, 25 g protein

Ingredients:

- ground turkey (1 lb.)
- jalapeño pepper, (3/4, minced)
- shallot (1 med., peeled and minced)
- Lime (1, zested with 2 tsp. juice)
- cilantro (2 tbsp., chopped)
- paprika (1 tsp.)
- cumin (1 tsp.)
- sea salt (1/2 tsp.)
- black pepper (1/2 tsp.)
- guacamole
- Pico de Gallo

Directions:

1. Add all your ingredients to a bowl then mix until it is fully combined. Form to make 4 patties.
2. Preheat a skillet with a little olive oil in it on medium heat. Cook the patties for 5 minutes per side, or until cooked through.
3. Serve with guacamole, Pico de Gallo or toppings of choice.

Crock Pot Thai Turkey Curry

Yields: 2   Prep: 10 mins.   Cook: 4 hrs.
Nutrition per Serving:
436 calories, 28 g fat, 24 g carbs, 3 g fiber, 28 g protein

Ingredients:

- ❖ water (2 cups)
- ❖ Thai red curry paste (2-4 tbsp., or to taste)
- ❖ soy sauce (1 tbsp.)
- ❖ minced ginger (1 tbsp.)
- ❖ fish sauce (2 tsp)
- ❖ garlic cloves (3, minced)
- ❖ turkey thighs (1 lb. boneless, skinless, cut into 2-3 pieces

- ❖ Kabocha squash (1 large, cut into 1 – inch cubes)
- ❖ yellow onion (1 medium, chopped)
- ❖ chili peppers (1-2, optional)
- ❖ coconut milk (1 14 oz can)
- ❖ Kale (1 bunch, torn)
- ❖ Cilantro and lime wedges for serving

Directions:

1. Add all the ingredients, with the exception of your coconut milk and kale in a slow cooker and mix well.
2. Cook on high for 4 hours and then stir in the coconut milk and kale.
3. Mix well and cook on high for another 15-20 minutes, or until hot through and the kale has wilted.
4. Season to taste with salt and pepper and serve with cilantro and lime wedges.

Creamy Sun-dried Tomato Turkey

Yields: 8   Prep: 15 mins.   Cook: 1 hr. 15 mins.

Nutrition per Serving:

162 calories, 8 g fat, 7 g carbs, 2 g fiber, 16 g protein

Ingredients:

- Salt (1 Tbs)
- Freshly Ground Pepper (1 tsp.)
- Turkey thighs (8, bone-in, skin removed)
- Extra Virgin Olive Oil (3 Tbs)
- Yellow Onion (1, sliced thinly)
- Sun-dried Tomatoes (¾ cup, sliced)
- Garlic (1 Tbs, minced)
- Italian Seasoning (1 tsp)
- large pinch Red Pepper Flakes
- Coconut Milk (13.5 oz can)
- Turkey Stock (1 cup)
- Basil shredded, to top

Directions:

1. Turn your oven on and allow to preheat up to 400 degrees F. Thoroughly season your turkey with your salt and pepper.
2. Fry the turkey, in an oven safe skillet, in the olive oil for 2-3 minutes, or until browned on all sides. Set aside.
3. Add a little more oil to the pan and sauté the onion for 2 minutes. Add the Italian seasoning, garlic, tomatoes and red pepper and cook for 30 seconds.
4. Stir in the coconut milk and chicken broth and bring the mixture to a boil. Place the turkey back into the sauce and spoon some sauce on top.
5. Cover and bake for 45 minutes. Reduce heat to 300 degrees F and cook for another 20 minutes. Garnish with basil before serving.

White Mushroom & Carrot Soup

Yields: 4   Prep: 15 mins.   Cook: 20 mins.
Nutrition per Serving:
219 calories, 12 g fat, 15 g carbs, 3 g fiber, 13 g protein

Ingredients:
- olive oil (2 tbs)
- carrots (2, chopped)
- white mushrooms (5 cups, sliced)
- smoked ham (1 ½ cups, diced)
- garlic powder (2 tsp)
- chicken broth (2 (14 oz) can)
- stewed tomatoes (1 (14 oz) can, seedless)

Directions:
1. Heat the oil up over medium heat, in a soup pot. Add carrots; cook, stir often, for 5 minutes.
2. Add mushrooms; cook, stirring frequently for 5 minutes. Add ham, garlic powder, chicken broth and tomatoes.
3. Bring to a boil; reduce heat and simmer covered for 10 minutes. Serve.

Shitake & Ginger Soup

Yields: 4   Prep: 20 mins.   Cook: 15 mins.
Nutrition per Serving:
117 calories, 3 g fat, 19 g carbs, 1 g fiber, 4g protein

Ingredients:
- vegetable oil (2 tsp)
- garlic cloves (3, crushed and peeled)
- fresh ginger (1 tbs, finely shredded)
- Shitake mushrooms (4 oz, sliced)
- vegetable stock (4 cups)
- light soy sauce (1 tsp, optional)
- bean sprouts (4 oz)
- thin spaghetti pasta (4 oz, white)
- fresh cilantro (4 tbs)

Directions:
1. Bring a salted water to boil in a pot. Add the pasta and cook as the package instructed.
2. While pasta is cooking, in a large soup pot, heat oil over medium heat. Add garlic, ginger and mushrooms.
3. Stir until softened, about 3-4 minutes. Add vegetable stock and bring to boil.
4. Add soy sauce and bean sprouts and continue to cook until tender. Serve and garnish with fresh cilantro.

Banana Cocoa Cream

Yields: 4   Prep: 4 hrs.   Cook: 0 mins.
Nutrition per Serving:
0.1 calories, 1 g fat, 7 g carbs, 1g fiber, 0 g protein

Ingredients:
- ❖ Banana (1, mashed)
- ❖ cocoa powder, to taste
- ❖ stevia, to taste (optional)

Directions:
1. Mix one mashed banana with stevia and cocoa powder. You may blend these together or use a food processor for best results.
2. Freeze in a sealed container for 2-4 hours.

Honey Banana Smoothie

Yields: 1   Prep: 15 mins.   Cook: 0 mins.
Nutrition per Serving:
471 calories, 8 g fat, 75 g carbs, 4 g fiber, 23g protein

Ingredients:
- ❖ Banana (1, medium)
- ❖ Milk (1 cup, low fat)
- ❖ Yogurt (1/2 cup, nonfat, plain)
- ❖ Refined cereal (1/4 cup)
- ❖ vanilla extract (1 tsp)
- ❖ honey (2 tsp)
- ❖ ice (1/2 cup)
- ❖ cinnamon (1 dash)

Directions:
1. In a blender put all ingredients and process until smooth. Garnish with cinnamon.

Oatmeal Cookie Smoothie

Yields: 1   Prep: 5 mins.   Cook: 0 mins.
Nutrition per Serving:
336 calories, 11 g fat, 54 g carbs, 5 g fiber, 10 g protein

Ingredients:

- yellow banana (1 sliced and frozen)
- milk (¾ cup)
- ice (¼ cup)
- rolled oats (2 tbsp.)
- almond butter (2 tsp.)
- vanilla (1/8 tsp.)
- cinnamon (½ tsp.)
- Small sprinkle ground nutmeg optional

Directions:
1. Add all your ingredients to your blender then allow to process until you achieve a smooth consistency.

Peach Smoothie

Yields: 1   Prep: 10 mins.   Cook: 0 mins.
Nutrition per Serving:
367 calories, 8 g fat, 44 g carbs, 2 g fiber, 23 g protein

Ingredients:

- Peaches (1/2 cup, peeled, cooked)
- milk (1 cup, non-fat)
- yogurt (1/2 cup, non-fat, peach flavoured)
- flakes (1/4 cup, refined cereal)
- vanilla extract (1 tsp)
- honey (1 tsp, optional)
- ice (1/2 cup)

Directions:
1. In a blender put all ingredients and process until smooth and creamy.

Homemade Pumpkin Pie

Yields: 10   Prep: 5 mins.   Cook: 45 mins.
Nutrition per Serving:
342 calories, 1 g fat, 42 g carbs, 1 g fiber, 5 g protein

Ingredients:
Crust:
- ❖ 1, half-batch All Butter Pie crust, fitted into a 9-inch, crimped and chilled

Filling:
- ❖ pumpkin purée (1, 15- ounce, can)
- ❖ sugar (¾ cup)
- ❖ eggs (2 large, at room temperature)
- ❖ lactose-free evaporated milk (11- ounces)
- ❖ cinnamon (1 teaspoon)
- ❖ ginger (½ teaspoon, ground)
- ❖ salt (1/4 teaspoon)
- ❖ cloves (¼ teaspoon, ground)

Directions:
1. Position rack in center of oven. Set oven to preheat to 425°F. Whisk eggs, sugar and pumpkin together in medium bowl.
2. Whisk in your salt, cinnamon, ginger, clove and evaporated milk until smooth.
3. Pour filling into the crust and bake in the oven for 15 minutes. Make sure to turn the temperature down to 340 F (170 C) and bake until the filling is set. This will take around 30 to 40 minutes.
4. You can serve the pie on the day it is baked. If you want to make it 1 day ahead before serving it make sure to store it at room temperature.

Chocolate Pear Cream

Yields: 4   Prep: 4 hrs.   Cook: 0 mins.
Nutrition per Serving:
96 calories, 1 g fat, 7 g carbs, 1 g fiber, 0g protein

Ingredients:
- Pear (1, cooked, mashed)
- cocoa powder, to taste
- stevia, to taste (optional)

Directions:
1. Mix one mashed pear with stevia and cocoa powder.
2. You may blend these together or use a food processor for best results. Freeze in a sealed container for 2-4 hours.

Zero Sugar Pumpkin Pie

Yields: 16   Prep: 10 mins.   Cook: 1 hr.
Nutrition per Serving:
84 calories, 3 g fat, 1 g carbs, 3 g fiber, 35 g protein

Ingredients:
- Pumpkin (1 15oz can)
- ground cinnamon (3/4 tsp.)
- ground nutmeg (1/2 tsp.)
- ground ginger (1/2 tsp)
- ground cloves (1/2 tsp.)
- Evaporated Skim Milk (1 14oz can)
- Eggs (2 large, slightly beaten)
- Splenda (1/2 cup)
- Pie Crust (9" deep dish, refined white flour)

Directions:
1. Baked at 350 degrees for 1 hour. Makes 16 small servings.

Orange Curd

Yields: 20   Prep:5 mins. Cook:15 mins.
Nutrition per Serving:
72 calories, 3 g fat, 12 g carbs, 1g fiber, 1 g protein

Ingredients:
- ❖ Butter (55g)
- ❖ Sugar (225g)
- ❖ Eggs (2 Large, beaten)

- ❖ Juice and finely grated zest of 2 oranges

Directions:
1. Put a bowl over a pan of simmering water and add the butter and sugar until dissolved. Add the orange zest and juice.
2. Gently whisk while adding the eggs. Let it cook gently stirring until it is thick and like custard this should take 15 minutes. Remove it from the heat and place it into a jar.

Instant Pot Pear Crumble

Yields: 6   Prep: 15 mins.   Cook: 25 mins.
Nutrition per Serving:
279 calories, 10 g fat, 48 g carbs, 1 g fiber, 2 g protein

Ingredients:
- ❖ pears (5 large, cut into 1-inch chunks)
- ❖ water (1/3 cup)
- ❖ flour (3 Tbsp)
- ❖ quick oats (¾ cup)

- ❖ coconut sugar (½ cup)
- ❖ ground cinnamon (2 tsp)
- ❖ fine sea salt (¼ tsp)
- ❖ melted coconut oil or butter (¼ cup)

Directions:
1. Add your water and pears into your Instant Pot and stir well to be sure the pears cover the bottom of the pot in an even layer.
2. In a separate bowl, combine salt, cinnamon, sugar, oats and flour then stir well.
3. Add the melted coconut oil and stir until thoroughly mixed. Top pears with crumble.
4. Select Manual/Pressure. Cook on high pressure for 8 minutes. Naturally release the pressure from your IP (about 10 minutes).
5. Remove the lid. Use oven mitts to remove the dish from the Instant Pot and let the crumble cool for 10 minutes before serving warm.

Sweet Potato Cream Pie

Yields: 4   Prep: 5 mins.   Cook: 16 mins.

Nutrition per Serving:

181 calories, 2 g fat, 18g carbs, 0g fiber, 35 g protein

Ingredients:

- water (1 cup)
- sweet potato (1, peeled and diced)
- coconut milk (½ cup full-fat canned)
- pure maple syrup (6 Tbsp, plus more as needed)
- fresh ginger (1 tsp, grated, about ½-inch knob)

Directions:

1. Add 1 cup water to the Instant Pot and arrange a steamer basket on the bottom. Place the sweet potato pieces in the steamer basket and cover.
2. Seal your steam valve. Set the IP on Pressure Cook or Manual mode then cook on High for 10 minutes.
3. When ready, immediately move the steam release valve to Venting to quickly release the steam pressure.
4. Use oven mitts to lift the steamer basket out of the pot and transfer the cooked potatoes to a large bowl.
5. Add the coconut milk, maple syrup, and ginger. Use an immersion blender or potato masher to puree the potatoes into a smooth pudding.
6. Taste and adjust the flavor, adding more ginger or maple syrup as needed. Serve the pudding right away, or chill it in the fridge.
7. Store leftover pudding in an airtight container in the fridge for 1 week.

Almond Peanut Butter Fudge

Yields: 2   Prep: 2 hrs.10 mins.   Cook: 0 mins.

Nutrition per Serving:

287calories, 30 g fat, 4 g carbs, 2g fiber, 5 g protein

Ingredients:

- ❖ peanut butter (1 cup, unsweetened)
- ❖ vanilla almond milk (1/4 cup, unsweetened)
- ❖ coconut oil (1 cup)
- ❖ vanilla liquid stevia (2 tsps., optional)
- ❖ Salt - pinch

For the Chocolate Sauce (topping):

- ❖ melted coconut oil (2 tbsps.)
- ❖ cocoa powder (1/4 cup, unsweetened)
- ❖ maple syrup (2 tbsps.)

Directions:

For Chocolate Sauce:

1. Take a bowl and add the coconut oil, maple syrup and cocoa powder
2. Whisk together completely and keep it aside.

For Peanut Butter Fudge:

3. Slightly melt the coconut oil and peanut butter together over low heat on the stove (you can also use the microwave).
4. Add this melted mixture, vanilla almond milk, stevia and salt to the blender. Blend well until thoroughly combined.
5. Pour this blended mixture to a loaf pan lined with a parchment. Refrigerate for 2 hours until set.
6. Drizzle the chocolate sauce over the fudge after it has been set. Refrigerate it for some more time and then serve.

Quick Cocoa Mousse

Yields: 8　　Prep: 10 mins.　　Cook: 0 mins.
Nutrition per Serving:
227 calories, 2 g fat, 3 g carbs, 1 g fiber, 4 g protein

Ingredients:

- heavy whipping cream (6 tbsps., whip it and keep ready)
- butter (4 tbsps., unsalted)
- cocoa powder (1 tbsp)
- cream cheese (4 tbsps.)
- coconut oil (1 tsp)
- Stevia (as per taste)

Directions:

1. Soften the butter in a microwave and then combine it with stevia. Stir well until it blends completely.
2. Add the cream cheese and cocoa powder to the butter mixture. Blend thoroughly until it becomes smooth.
3. Slowly add the whipped heavy cream to the mixture and keep stirring. Add 1 tsp of MCT oil or coconut oil to the mixture and blend again.
4. Spoon the smooth mixture into small glasses and refrigerate for 30 minutes. Serve chilled.

Cinnamon Pear Chips

Yields: 4   Prep: 5 mins.   Cook: 3 hrs.
Nutrition per Serving:
96 calories, 0 g fat, 26 g carbs, 1 g fiber, 1 g protein

Ingredients:
- Pears (4)
- ground cinnamon (1 teaspoon)

Directions:
1. Preheat the oven to 200°F. Line a baking sheet with parchment paper.
2. Core the pears and cut into ⅛-inch slices. Toss pears with cinnamon.
3. Spread the pears in a single layer on the prepared baking sheet. Cook for 2 to 3 hours, until the pears are dry.
4. They will still be soft while hot but will crisp once completely cooled. Store in an airtight container for up to four days.

Chocolate Yogurt Cream & Roasted Bananas

Yields: 4   Prep: 10 mins.   Cook: 5 mins.
Nutrition per Serving:
236 calories, 0 g fat, 42g carbs, 3 g fiber, 7 g protein

Ingredients:
- whipping cream (½ cup)
- ground cinnamon (½ tsp)
- low fat vanilla yogurt (1 ½ cups, chilled and drained)
- cold butter (1 tbsp)
- confectioner's sugar (1 tbsp)
- dark rum (1 tbsp)
- unsweetened cocoa powder (2 tbsp)
- dark brown sugar (3 tbsp)
- bananas (4, cut in strips)

Directions:
1. Place bananas cut side up on a baking sheet coated with cooking spray.
2. Sprinkle with brown sugar, rum and cinnamon. Dot with butter.
3. Roast in a 425-degree Fahrenheit preheated oven for five minutes. Turn the broiler off until the bananas are golden.
4. Meanwhile, beat the cocoa, cream and confectioner's sugar in a large bowl using an electric mixer.
5. Add the drained yogurt and fold the cream until well combined. Plate the roasted bananas and add a dollop of chocolate cream on top.

Coconut Celery Smoothie

Yields: 2   Prep: 10 mins.   Cook: 0 mins.
Nutrition per Serving:
391 calories, 15 g fat, 42 g carbs, 1 g fiber, 29 g protein

Ingredients:
- celery stalks (3, shredded)
- ground cinnamon (1 tsp)
- banana (½)
- protein powder (1 scoop)
- coconut butter (1 tbsp)
- unsweetened coconut milk (1 cup)

Directions:
1. Toss your ingredients into a blender then process until creamy and smooth. Serve immediately and enjoy.

Apple Spinach Smoothie

Yields: 2   Prep: 10 mins.   Cook: 0 mins.
Nutrition per Serving:
388 calories, 19 g fat, 43 g carbs, 3 g fiber, 15 g protein

Ingredients:
- vanilla extract (¼ tsp)
- ginger (1 tsp, grated)
- maple syrup (1 tsp)
- coconut butter (1 ½ tbsp)
- yogurt (½ cup)
- apple (1, chopped)
- baby spinach (1 cup)
- unsweetened coconut milk (1 cup)

Directions:
1. Toss your ingredients into a blender then process until creamy and smooth. Serve immediately and enjoy.

High Fiber Breakfast Ideas

Pear Turkey Pita

Yields: 4   Prep: 15 mins.   Cook: 0 mins.
Nutrition per Serving:
221 calories, 3 g fat, 21 g carbs, 2 g fiber, 25 g protein

Ingredients:
- Turkey (2 cups, cooked, cubed)
- Pears (2, medium, unpeeled, chopped)
- Celery (1 stalk, chopped)
- Yogurt (1/3 cup, plain, low fat or non-fat)
- Mayonnaise (1/4 cup, non-fat)
- pita breads (4, round, whole wheat)
- lettuce leaves (4, romaine)

Directions:
1. In a bowl, combine the turkey, celery, and pears. Add mayonnaise and yogurt then combine. Create a pocket by slicing pita.
2. Put the lettuce leaf inside the pita and fill the pocket with 1 cup of mixture in each pita bread.
3. Serve with mixed fruits. Do not include berries).

Overnight Oats

Yields: 4   Prep: 5 mins.   Cook: 0 mins.
Nutrition per Serving:
267 calories, 16 g fat, 34 g carbs, 4 g fiber, 4g protein

Ingredients:
- Almond Milk (1 cup)
- Fruit of choice (1/2 cup)
- Gluten-free Oats (1 cup)
- ½ tbsp Honey

Directions:
1. Mix 1 cup oats with 2/3 cup almond milk. Add fruit and honey.
2. Leave in refrigerator overnight in a mason jar or similar sealable container. Mix well in the morning before eating.

Veggie Scramble

Yields: 1   Prep: 5 mins.   Cook: 0 mins.
Nutrition per Serving:
157 calories, 6 g fat, 15 g carbs, 6 g fiber, 16 g protein

Ingredients:
- Eggs (2)
- Spinach (1 cup)
- Tomato (1 medium)
- Spices of your choice (to taste)
- Cooking spray

Directions:
1. Mix eggs, spinach, and chopped tomato in a bowl.
2. Spray a pan with cooking spray and pour bowl contents onto pan when hot. Cook until eggs are no longer runny.

Turkey and Avocado Pitas

Yields: 4   Prep: 10 mins.   Cook: 0 mins.

Nutrition per Serving:

277 calories, 11 g fat, 10 g carbs, 4 g fiber, 30 g protein

Ingredients:

- ❖ Turkey (2 cups, cooked, cubed)
- ❖ avocado (1 medium, chopped)
- ❖ red beans (1 (14 oz.) can, drained and rinsed)
- ❖ lemon juice (1 tsp)
- ❖ tomatoes (1 cup, seeded, chopped)
- ❖ low fat cottage cheese (1 cup)
- ❖ whole wheat pita bread (4 round)

Directions:

1. In a large mixing bowl, combine turkey, avocado, red beans, lemon juice, tomatoes, and cottage cheese.
2. Slice the pita bread to make a pocket and spoon in the turkey mixture. Serve.

Grilled Vegetable Sandwich

Yields: 4   Prep: 10 mins.   Cook: 12 mins.
Nutrition per Serving:
681 calories, 66 g fat, 14 g carbs, 6 g fiber, 16 g protein

Ingredients:

- Japanese eggplant (1, sliced in half-inch thick slices)
- Zucchini (1 small, sliced in half-inch thick slices)
- red pepper (1, seeded and quartered)
- Portobello mushroom caps (2)
- extra-virgin olive oil (1/2 cup)
- salt (1/4 tsp)
- goat cheese (6 oz)
- whole wheat (8 slices)
- baby spinach (1 cup)

Directions:

1. With a pastry brush, brush olive oil on the vegetable slices and the mushrooms caps.
2. Season them with salt. Put the vegetables on the grill and cook it until they are tender.
3. To assemble, slice the mushrooms, spread goat cheese on both sides of the bread.
4. Add the grilled vegetables of each variation and a quarter of the mushrooms.
5. Cover with spinach and top with bread before serving.

Spinach and Ham Pizza

Yields: 4   Prep: 10 mins.   Cook: 12 mins.

Nutrition per Serving:

256 calories, 19 g fat, 4 g carbs, 1 g fiber, 18 g protein

Ingredients:

- store-bought baked thin-crust whole wheat pizza shell (1)
- baby spinach leaves (4 cups, thinly sliced)
- olive oil (2 teaspoons)
- ham (3 ounces, thinly sliced)
- Feta cheese (1/4, crumbled)
- Parmesan cheese (1/4 cup grated)
- cloves (3, thinly sliced garlic)

Directions:

1. Preheat oven to 450F degrees. Place the pizza shell on a cookie sheet.
2. Scatter spinach all over crust. Drizzle with oil. Place ham, garlic, and cheeses on top of spinach.
3. Bake for 10-12 minutes, until spinach is wilted.

Fruit Bowl

Yields: 4   Prep: 5 mins.   Cook: 0 mins.

Nutrition per Serving:

308 calories, 1 g fat, 79g carbs, 13 g fiber, 4 g protein

Ingredients:

- Pears (1 cup, cut in half-inch cubes)
- Bananas (1 cup, cut in half-inch cubes)
- Oranges (1 cup, cut in half-inch cubes)

Directions:

1. Mix all ingredients together and serve with a salad dressing.

Easy Tofu & Beans

Yields: 4   Prep: 15 mins.   Cook: 20 mins.

Nutrition per Serving:

678 calories, 44 g fat, 55g carbs, 6g fiber, 19g protein

Ingredients:

- ❖ firm tofu (1 (14 oz) pkg., drained, cut in cubes)
- ❖ whole wheat flour (1/4 cup)
- ❖ canola oil (1 tbs)
- ❖ olive oil (1/2 cup)
- ❖ balsamic vinegar (2 tbs)
- ❖ Dijon mustard (1 tbs)
- ❖ soy sauce (3 tbs)

- ❖ onions (1/2 cup, sliced)
- ❖ carrots (1/2 cups, sliced)
- ❖ green beans (1 cup, ends cut)
- ❖ fresh soybeans (1/2 cups)
- ❖ cabbage (1 1/2 cups, chopped)
- ❖ brown rice (1 cup, cooked)

Directions:

1. In a shallow bowl or plate, mix tofu with flour until evenly coated. Heat up the canola oil over medium heat, in a non-stick pan.
2. Add tofu and cook until lightly brown. Remove from pan and put aside.
3. Prepare dressing by whisking together olive oil, vinegar, mustard and soy sauce.
4. In same pan, combine 2 tablespoons of the dressing mixture with onions, carrots, green beans, soybeans and cabbage.
5. Stir fry for 10 minutes. Add remaining dressing mixture and tofu. Mix. Cook for 2 minutes, stirring gently.
6. Serve over hot brown rice.

Couscous with Dates

Yields: 4   Prep: 10 mins.   Cook: 10 mins.
Nutrition per Serving:
197 calories, 4 g fat, 33g carbs, 2 g fiber, 6 g protein

Ingredients:

- Water (1/2 cup)
- turkey stock (1 cup)
- olive oil (1 tbs)
- dried dates (1/2 cup, chopped)

- couscous (1 cup)
- spinach (1 cup, chopped)
- lemon juice (1/2 tsp)
- salt (1/2 tsp)

Directions:

1. In a medium saucepan, over high heat, bring water, chicken broth, oil and dates to a boil. Remove from heat and stir in couscous.
2. Cover and let sit for 5-10 minutes. Stir in spinach into couscous. Add lemon juice and salt and fluff together with a fork. Serve.

Pork Fajitas

Yields: 4   Prep: 10 mins.   Cook: 15 mins.
Nutrition per Serving:
286 calories, 13 g fat, 10 g carbs, 2 g fiber, 32 g protein

Ingredients:

- flank steak (5 oz, trimmed of excess fat)
- lime juice (2 tsp)
- garlic (1 tsp, chopped)
- extra virgin olive oil (1 tsp, divided)
- can red beans (1 (15 oz), drained and rinsed)
- green bell pepper (1/2 cup, thinly sliced)
- red bell pepper (1/2 cup, thinly sliced)
- scallions (1 tbsp, chopped finely)
- Salt to taste
- whole wheat tortillas (4)

Directions:

1. Season flank steak with salt. Let sit for 10 minutes. Put the flank steak on the grill over high heat until cooked on both sides.
2. Transfer to a new plate to rest (about 10 minutes). Slice steak against the grain.
3. In a small bowl, whisk together lime juice, garlic, and olive oil. Set aside.
4. In a separate bowl, combine beans, bell peppers and scallions and season with salt. To assemble, place your steak inside your tortillas.
5. Add your bean mixture on top then sprinkle with lime sauce. Roll into fajita and serve immediately.

Cottage Crunch Wraps

Yields: 2   Prep: 10 mins.   Cook: 0 mins.
Nutrition per Serving:
194 calories, 3 g fat, 24 g carbs, 4 g fiber, 19 g protein

Ingredients:
- cottage cheese (3/4 cup)
- carrots (1/4 cup, grated)
- green onions (1/4 cup, sliced finely)
- tomatoes (1/2 cup, seeded and chopped)
- cabbage (1/2 cup, chopped)
- lime juice (1 teaspoon)
- whole wheat tortillas (2 round)

Directions:
1. In a bowl, place cheese, carrots, onions, cabbage, and tomatoes and mix well. Add lime juice. Place mixture in tortillas, wrap and serve.

Bean & Vegetable Pasta

Yields: 4   Prep: 10 mins.   Cook: 26 mins.
Nutrition per Serving:
232 calories, 16 g fat, 17g carbs, 3 g fiber, 17 g protein

Ingredients:

- whole wheat penne pasta (1 lb)
- olive oil (2 tbs)
- cloves garlic (2, minced)
- tomatoes (3 cups, seeded and chopped)
- cannellini beans (1 (14 oz) can, drained and rinsed)
- tomato sauce (1 cup)
- spinach (2 cups, washed and chopped)
- crumbled feta cheese (1/2 cup)

Directions:

1. Bring a salted water to boil in a pot. Add the pasta then ensure to follow the cooking instructions on the package. Then drain it.
2. Set your oil to get hot on medium heat in a nonstick pan. Cook garlic for 3 - 4 minutes. Add tomatoes, beans and tomato sauce.
3. Bring to a boil. Reduce the heat, cover and let simmer for 10 minutes. Add spinach to the sauce and let simmer for another 5 minutes or until spinach wilts.
4. Transfer to a large bowl. Combine with your sauce the top with feta. Toss to combine. Serve.

Vegetarian Penne Pasta

Yields: 2   Prep: 10 mins.   Cook: 16 mins.
Nutrition per Serving:
283 calories, 17 g fat, 26 g carbs, 4g fiber, 10 g protein

Ingredients:
- whole wheat penne (1/2 lb)
- salt (1 tbs)
- extra virgin olive oil (2 tbs)
- white mushrooms (8 oz sliced)
- asparagus (8 oz, chopped thawed)
- red bell pepper (8 oz, seeded and chopped)
- Parmesan cheese (1/4 cup, grated)
- fresh basil (1/4 cup, chopped)

Directions:
1. Bring a salted water to boil in a pot. Add pasta and cook until it is al dente or follow the instructions on the package.
2. While the pasta is cooking, in a medium pan, heat olive oil over medium heat. Add the mushrooms and cook for five minutes.
3. Add the bell pepper and asparagus. Sauté for 4 minutes. Add the cooked pasta in the pan and add cheese, stir until well combined.
4. Put the mixture in a serving bowl, garnish with basil and serve.

Black Bean Pita Pockets

Yields: 4   Prep: 20 mins.   Cook: 0 mins.
Nutrition per Serving:
54 calories, 1 g fat, 11 g carbs, 4 g fiber, 3 g protein

Ingredients:

- Black beans (1 (15 oz) can, rinsed and drained)
- artichoke hearts (1 (6 oz) can, marinated, quartered, liquid reserved)
- black olives (1 tbs, sliced)
- green olives (1 tbs, sliced)
- green bell pepper (1 small, seeded and diced)
- red bell pepper (1 small, seeded and diced)
- red onion (1 small, thinly sliced)
- red wine vinegar (2 tbs)
- basil (1/2 cup, chopped)
- whole wheat pita bread (4 large)
- leaves lettuce (4)

Directions:
1. In a bowl, combine the artichokes, Black beans and their liquid, basil, garlic, vinegar, peppers, onion, and olives.
2. Set aside after you mix well. Slice the pita bread so that it can make a pocket. Place a lettuce in each pita and fill with the Black filling.
3. Serve.

Vegetarian Bean Curry

Yields: 4   Prep: 15 mins.   Cook: 40 mins.

Nutrition per Serving:

531 calories, 12 g fat, 19 g carbs, 18 g fiber, 19 g protein

Ingredients:

- ❖ vegetable oil (2 tablespoons)
- ❖ onion (1, sliced)
- ❖ curry powder (2 tbs, mild)
- ❖ garlic powder (1/2 tsp)
- ❖ ginger (1/4 tsp, grated)
- ❖ tomatoes (1 (15 oz) can, seeded and diced)
- ❖ garbanzo beans (2 (15 oz) cans)
- ❖ potatoes (2 cups, unpeeled, diced)
- ❖ carrots (1 cup, sliced)
- ❖ cauliflower pieces (1 (16 oz) package frozen)
- ❖ peas (1 (10 oz) package frozen)
- ❖ Water as necessary
- ❖ salt (1/4 tsp)
- ❖ hot brown rice (2 cups cooked)

Directions:

1. Heat up the oil over medium heat in a non-stick pan. Cook onions until softened.
2. Add curry powder, ginger and garlic powder; cook 2 minutes. Add the tomatoes, garbanzo beans, carrots, and potatoes and stir together.
3. Add cauliflower, cover and reduce heat to simmer. Cook for 20-30 minutes, until vegetable is tender, adding water if necessary.
4. Stir in peas and salt; cook 5 more minutes. Serve over hot rice.

Bean Enchiladas

Yields: 4   Prep: 15 mins.   Cook: 20 mins.

Nutrition per Serving:

231 calories, 2 g fat, 51 g carbs, 13 g fiber, 12 g protein

Ingredients:

- ❖ Red beans, (1, 14 oz can, drained rinsed and mashed)
- ❖ low- fat cheddar cheese, (2 cups, shredded)
- ❖ onion (1/2 cup, chopped)
- ❖ black olives, (1/4 cup)
- ❖ tomato sauce (2 cups)
- ❖ garlic salt (2 tsp)
- ❖ whole wheat tortillas (8 medium)

Directions:

1. Preheat oven to 350F degrees. In a bowl, combine one cup tomato sauce, garlic salt, onions, olives, cheese, and mashed beans.
2. Place 1/3 cup bean along center of each tortilla. Place the enchiladas in baking dish after it has been rolled.
3. Place the tomato sauce on top of the already filled tortillas. If desired, sprinkle with more cheese.
4. Bake for 20 minutes or until thoroughly heated.

Bean Vegetable Casserole

Yields: 4   Prep: 30 mins.   Cook: 1 hr. 30 mins.

Nutrition per Serving:

459 calories, 9 g fat, 76g carbs, 19 g fiber, 22 g protein

Ingredients:

- vegetable oil (3 tbs)
- onion, (1 large, chopped)
- celery, (2 stalks, chopped)
- green bell pepper (1 med, seeded and diced)
- tomatoes (2 med, seeded and diced)
- red kidney beans (2 cups, drained and rinsed)
- baby lima beans (2 1/4 cups, frozen and thawed)
- barley (1 cup)
- Italian parsley (2/3 cup, chopped)
- Salt (1/2 tsp)
- dried basil (1 tsp)
- cumin (1/2 tsp)
- boiling water (1 3/4 cups)

Directions:

1. Preheat oven to 350F degrees. In a non-stick pan, heat up the oil over medium heat. Add onion, celery, and green pepper.
2. Cook for 10 minutes or until vegetables soften. Stir the basil, lima beans, salt, barley, kidney beans, parsley, tomatoes, and cumin.
3. Take the mixture out of the pan and put it in a 3-quart casserole dish.
4. Ensure that the casserole dish has been sprayed with cooking spray that is not stick.
5. Add boiling water. Cover. Bake at 350 degrees for 1-1/2 hours.

Black Bean Quesadillas

Yields: 4   Prep: 10 mins.   Cook: 12 mins.

Nutrition per Serving:

203 calories, 1 g fat, 37 g carbs, 9 g fiber, 12 g protein

Ingredients:

- black beans (1 (28 oz) can, drained and rinsed)
- tomatoes (1/2 cup, seeded and chopped)
- cilantro (3 tbs, chopped)
- black olives (1/2 cup, pitted, halved)
- cumin (1/2 tsp)
- fat free Monterey Jack cheese (1/2 cup, shredded)
- fresh spinach leaves (2 cups, shredded)
- whole wheat tortillas (8 round)

Directions:

1. Preheat oven to 350 degrees. In a bowl, mash beans until smooth, but, slightly chunky.
2. Stir in tomato, cilantro and olives and cumin. Spread mixture evenly onto 4 tortillas. Sprinkle with cheese, and spinach.
3. Put the remaining tortillas on top. Bake the tortillas on a baking sheet that is not greased for 12 minutes.
4. Cut into wedges and serve.

Broccoli and Mushroom Rice

Yields: 4   Prep: 15 mins.   Cook: 25 mins.

Nutrition per Serving:

231 calories, 5 g fat, 41 g carbs, 3 g fiber, 6 g protein

Ingredients:

- extra virgin olive oil (1 tbs)
- onion (1 medium, chopped)
- cloves garlic (2, minced)
- instant brown rice (1 cup)
- Portobello mushroom (8 oz., sliced)
- vegetable stock (3/4 cup)
- fresh broccoli florets (1 lb)
- salt (1/2 tsp)

Directions:

1. Preheat oven to 350F degrees. Set oil over medium heat in a nonstick pan to get hot.
2. Cook onions and garlic until soft, about 5 minutes. Stir in rice and mushrooms and cook 3-5 minutes or until mushrooms have released all of their juices.
3. Add the broth and bring to a boil. Reduce heat to medium-low and cover until liquid is absorbed (about 7 - 8 minutes).
4. Place broccoli in a casserole dish and sprinkle with salt and add 4 tbs. water.
5. Cover and cook at high power for 5 to 7 minutes or until tender. Place rice into a serving platter and top with broccoli.
6. Toss to combine and serve.

Vegetable Curry

Yields: 4   Prep: 10 mins.   Cook: 20 mins.
Nutrition per Serving:
298 calories, 28 g fat, 14 g carbs, 5 g fiber, 4 g protein

Ingredients:
- butternut squash (1 ½ lbs., seeded and chopped)
- olive oil (1 tbs)
- onion (1 small, finely sliced)
- curry powder (1 tbs, mild)
- coconut milk (1 2/3 cups)
- water (1 cup)
- fresh spinach (3 cups, chopped)
- butter beans (1 (14 oz) can, drained and rinsed)
- fresh cilantro (2 tbs, chopped)

Directions:
1. Add your squash with enough water to cover it in a saucepan then boil under tender. Drain and set aside.
2. Set a deep pot on medium heat with oil to get hot. Once hot, add in onions and cook until fragrant.
3. Add in your curry and stir for about 3 minutes being careful not to let it burn.
4. Add your water and coconut milk and allow to come to a boil. Reduce heat, and simmer, without the cover, until thickened (about another 5 minutes).
5. Add in your remaining ingredients and stir until it's all heated through. Enjoy!

Chipotle Black Bean Chili

Yields: 4   Prep: 10 mins.   Cook: 30 mins.
Nutrition per Serving:
60 calories, 4 g fat, 6g carbs, 2 g fiber, 1 g protein

Ingredients:
- olive oil (1 tbs)
- onion (1 cup, finely chopped)
- cloves garlic (4, minced)
- chipotle powder (1/2 tsp)
- cumin (1/2 tsp)
- salt (1/4 tsp)
- black beans (1 (30 oz) can, drained and rinsed)
- tomatoes (1 (28 oz) can, diced and seedless)
- fresh cilantro (1 tsp)

Directions:
1. In a large non-stick pan, heat olive oil over medium heat. Add onions and garlic and cook 5 minutes or until they are soft.
2. Add in your tomatoes, beans, salt, cumin and chipotle powder then allow to boil.
3. Switch your heat to low, cover and allow to simmer until chili thickens (about 20 mins). Garnish with fresh cilantro. Serve.

Quinoa Stew

Yields: 4   Prep: 15 mins.   Cook: 40 mins.
Nutrition per Serving:
240 calories, 4 g fat, 38 g carbs, 17 g fiber, 14 g protein

Ingredients:
- vegetable oil (1 tbs)
- onion (1 large, chopped)
- cloves garlic (2, finely chopped)
- green bell pepper (1 med, chopped)
- water (3 cups or broth)
- Quinoa (1 1/4 cups, uncooked, rinsed)
- tomato sauce (1 can)
- oregano (½ tsp)
- thyme (½ tsp)
- basil (½ tsp)
- paprika (½ tsp)

Directions:
1. Heat the oil up over medium heat in a saucepan. Cook onion, bell pepper, and garlic, stir often, until vegetables are tender.
2. Stir in water, Quinoa, tomato sauce and spices. Turn the heat down low and cover it partially and let simmer 40 minutes or until Quinoa are tender. Serve.

Vegetable Couscous

Yields: 4   Prep: 5 mins.   Cook: 0 mins.
Nutrition per Serving:
396 calories, 18 g fat, 48g carbs, 6 g fiber, 12 g protein

Ingredients:
- vegetable stock (1 1/2 cups)
- couscous (1 cup, plain)
- olive oil (4 tbs, divided)
- red onion (1, chopped)
- cloves garlic (2, minced)
- tomatoes (3 large, seeded and diced)
- yellow bell pepper (1, seeded and chopped)
- red bell pepper (1, seeded and chopped)
- zucchinis (2, seeded and chopped)
- peas (1 cup, frozen and thawed)
- balsamic vinegar (2 tbs)
- feta cheese (2 tbs, crumbled)

Directions:
1. In a saucepan, over high heat, bring a tbs of olive oil and vegetable stock to a boil. Remove from heat and stir in couscous.
2. Cover and let sit for 5-10 minutes. In another pan over medium heat, add the remaining oil and cook the garlic and onions until softened.
3. Mix in the zucchini, tomatoes and bell peppers then continue to stir until tender.
4. Stir in your peas and continue to cook for another 3 more minutes.
5. Add in your cheese and vinegar then toss to combine.
6. Pour the vegetable mixture over couscous. Serve.

Quinoa Spaghetti Stew

Yields: 4　　Prep: 15 mins.　　Cook: 45 mins.

Nutrition per Serving:

393 calories, 12 g fat, 55g carbs, 17 g fiber, 18 g protein

Ingredients:

- olive oil (3 tbs)
- onion (1 large, chopped)
- cloves garlic (4, minced)
- carrots (3, chopped)
- celery stalks (3, chopped)
- Quinoa (1 cup, uncooked)
- water (2 1/2 quarts)
- salt (2 tsp)
- bay leaf (1)
- linguine (1/4 lb, broken into 1 1/2-inch pieces)
- kale (2 cups, chopped)
- Italian parsley (1/2 cup, chopped)

Directions:

1. Heat the olive oil over moderate heat in a pot. Cook the onion, garlic, and carrots and celery for 10 minutes, stirring occasionally, until tender.
2. Add the Quinoa, water, salt, and bay leaf to the pot. Bring to a boil.
3. Turn the heat down so that the content can simmer, cover the pot partially, stir often for 15 minutes.
4. Add the linguine and let it simmer, stir often, cook the Quinoa, kale and pasta until they are tender, 15 to 20 minutes longer.
5. Stir parsley into the stew. Serve

Quinoa Stir Fry

Yields: 4   Prep: 10 mins.   Cook: 13 mins.

Nutrition per Serving:

91 calories, 5 g fat, 10 g carbs, 4 g fiber, 3 g protein

Ingredients:

- sugar snap peas (1 cup)
- olive oil (2 tbs)
- onion (1 small, chopped)
- mushrooms (8 oz., sliced)
- artichoke hearts (1 (8 oz) can, drained)
- green Quinoa (1 (8 oz) can, drained)
- half and half cream (4 tbs)
- salt (1/2 tsp)

Directions:

1. Bring a small saucepan of water to boil. Once the water is boiling add sugar snap peas and add the salt. Once you do that make sure to turn off the heat and wait for 5 minutes. Drain the sugar snap peas under the water and set aside.
2. Drain the content under cold water, dry it with paper towel. Set aside.
3. In a pean heat an oil of your choice (I like to use olive oil) and fry onions for 4-5 minutes. Add mushrooms as well and stir for another 3-4 minutes.
4. Add sugar snap peas, artichoke and lentils while also adding cream, salt and pepper and fry for another 2-3 minutes.
5. Voila, ready to serve.

Grilled Vegetable Quesadillas

Yields: 2-4   Prep: 12 mins.   Cook: 8 mins.

Nutrition per Serving:

57 calories, 1 g fat, 12 g carbs, 3 g fiber, 4 g protein

Ingredients:

- Zucchini (1 small)
- yellow squash (1 small)
- yellow onion (1 small)
- red pepper (1, seeded)
- Portobello mushroom (1 small)
- oregano (1/2 tsp)
- salt (1/4 tsp)
- whole wheat tortillas (2)
- low fat Mozzarella cheese (1/2 cup, shredded)

Directions:

1. Over medium heat grill vegetables until all of the vegetables are cooked. Season with oregano and salt.
2. Slice vegetables and toss together. Heat a non-stick pan sprayed with non-stick cooking spray over medium heat and place one tortilla in the pan.
3. Spread some of the vegetable mixture over the tortilla, sprinkle with cheese and top with the remaining tortilla.
4. Turn tortilla over and heat the other side until cheese melts but do not brown the tortillas. Serve.

Quick Broccoli Pasta

Yields: 2   Prep: 8 mins.   Cook: 8 mins.
Nutrition per Serving:
246 calories, 11 g fat, 29g carbs, 5 g fiber, 11 g protein

Ingredients:
- broccoli florets (2 cups)
- whole wheat pasta (1/2 lb)
- extra virgin olive oil (1/2 tbs)
- parmesan cheese (1 1/2 tbs, grated)
- garlic powder (1/8 tsp)

Directions:
1. Bring a salted water to boil in a pot. Add in pasta and broccoli then cook until tender (about 8 minutes).
2. Drain well. In a large shallow pasta bowl put the pasta mixture and toss with olive oil, garlic powder and cheese. Serve.

Caribbean Rice & Pea

Yields: 4-6   Prep: 15 mins.   Cook: 15 mins.
Nutrition per Serving:
164 calories, 3 g fat, 27g carbs, 7 g fiber, 9 g protein

Ingredients:
- olive oil (1 tbs)
- onion (1 medium, chopped)
- sticks celery (2, chopped)
- cloves garlic (2, chopped)
- tomato paste (1 (14 oz) can)
- oregano (1/2 tsp)
- thyme (1/2 tsp)
- vegetable stock (1(14 oz) can)
- red beans (1 (28 oz) can, drained and rinsed)

Directions:
1. In a large non-stick pan, heat olive oil over medium heat. Cook onions, celery and garlic stirring until just tender.
2. Stir in tomato paste, oregano and thyme. Add stock, stir and bring to a boil.
3. Simmer uncovered about 15 minutes or until mixture thickens. Add red beans and let cook until heated through. Serve over rice.

Quinoa Risotto

Yields: 4   Prep: 15 mins.   Cook: 10 mins.
Nutrition per Serving:
457 calories, 9 g fat, 73g carbs, 17 g fiber, 21g protein

Ingredients:

- olive oil (2 tbs.)
- leeks (4 medium, chopped)
- cloves garlic (3, minced)
- red pepper (1 medium, seeded, finely chopped)
- vegetable stock (3 cups) brown rice (1 1/4 cup)
- basil (1 tbs, chopped)
- Quinoa (1 cup, cooked)
- Italian parsley (1/4 cup, chopped)
- fresh parmesan cheese (1/4 cup, grated)

Directions:

1. In a large pot, heat olive oil over moderate heat and cook leeks, garlic, and red pepper until softened.
2. Add stock along with the rice, and basil. Cover and let simmer until rice is done then add cooked Quinoa and stir for 10 minutes.
3. Remove from heat and add parsley and parmesan cheese. Serve.

Mushroom and Bean Stew

Yields: 4   Prep: 15 mins.   Cook: 22 mins.
Nutrition per Serving:
261 calories, 9 g fat, 33g carbs, 13 g fiber, 15 g protein

Ingredients:
- olive oil (2 tbs)
- white mushrooms (1 lb, sliced)
- onions (1 cup, chopped)
- garlic (1 tsp, minced)
- dried thyme (3/4 tsp)
- vegetable stock (2 (14 oz) cans)
- stewed tomatoes (1 (14 oz) can, chopped)
- dry white wine (1/4 cup)
- cannellini beans (30 oz., canned)

Directions:
1. Heat up the oil over medium heat in a saucepan. Cook the mushrooms, onion, thyme and garlic for about 7 minutes.
2. Bring to a boil when you add vegetable stock, wine and tomatoes.
3. Cover and simmer for about 15 additional minutes. In a bowl, mash up at least 1 cup of the beans until it has a smooth consistency; add the mashed beans into the stew.
4. Stir the rest of the beans, heat until hot. Serve immediately.

Quinoa & Brown Rice Bowl

Yields: 6   Prep: 15 mins.   Cook: 32 mins.

Nutrition per Serving:
307 calories, 7 g fat, 48g carbs, 12 g fiber, 14 g protein

Ingredients:
- olive oil (2 tbs.)
- onion (1, chopped)
- carrots (2, finely chopped)
- bell pepper (1, chopped)
- garlic clove (1, minced)
- dried basil (1 tbs)
- dried sage (1 tsp)
- brown rice (1 cup)
- vegetable stock (3 cups)
- Quinoa (1 cup, uncooked and rinsed)

Directions:
1. Heat up the olive oil over medium heat in a pan. Cook pepper onion and carrot until soft (about 6 minutes).
2. Add garlic and cook for one more minute. Add basil, sage and rice. Stir to combine.
3. Stir in broth. Bring to a boil, stirring occasionally. Add Quinoa.
4. Close the lid then switch to low heat. Simmer for another 20 minutes. Fluff with fork and serve.

Vegetarian Rice Casserole

Yields: 4   Prep: 20 mins.   Cook: 30 mins.
Nutrition per Serving:
57 calories, 1 g fat, 9g carbs, 2 g fiber, 4 g protein

Ingredients:

- Non-stick cooking spray
- long-grain brown rice (1 cup)
- fresh mushrooms (1/4 cup, sliced)
- broccoli (1/4 cup, chopped)
- carrots (1/4 cup, chopped)
- red bell pepper (1/4 cup, seeded and chopped)
- onion (1/4 cup, finely chopped)
- salt (1 tsp)
- paprika (1 tsp)
- oregano (1 tsp)
- vegetable stock (2 -1/2 cups)
- fat free cheddar cheese (1/4 cup, shredded)

Directions:
1. Preheat oven to 425 degrees. Lightly grease a glass baking dish (13x9) with cooking spray.
2. Mix the broccoli, brown rice, carrots, mushrooms, bell pepper, salt, onion, paprika, oregano, and broth.
3. Mix well and cover with foil. Bake until cooked through (about 30 minutes); stirring when the baking is halfway.
4. Add the cheese on top and allow it to melt prior to serving.

Pork and Penne Pasta

Yields: 4   Prep: 20 mins.   Cook: 30 mins.
Nutrition per Serving:
206 calories, 9 g fat, 24g carbs, 13 g fiber, 17 g protein

Ingredients:

- whole wheat penne pasta (1 lb.)
- ground Pork lean (1 lb)
- extra virgin olive oil (2 tbs)
- onion (1 small, chopped)
- garlic cloves (2, minced)
- can tomatoes (1 (15 oz), diced, seeded)
- green zucchini (2 cups sliced to 1/4 cubes)
- baby spinach (8 oz., fresh, chopped)
- low fat parmesan cheese (1 cup, grated)

Directions:

1. Bring a pot of water to a boil, ensure that the water is salted. Cook the pasta to an al dente consistency or according to package directions.
2. In a non-stick pan, cook the ground Pork over medium heat for 8 minutes or until it is browned, ensure to break up any large pieces in the pan.
3. Remove Pork and set aside. Discard drippings. Add in your oil on medium heat.
4. Cook onions and garlic for about 5 minutes or until soft. Add tomatoes and zucchini and continue cooking 5 minutes more.
5. Add spinach and cook until it just wilts, 2-3 minutes. Place the Pork back into the skillet and add 1/2 cup cheese; stir and heat through.
6. Plate your pasta then top with your meat mixture. Toss well and top evenly with cheese.

Chicken and Quinoa Pita

Yields: 4   Prep: 10 mins.   Cook: 0 mins.

Nutrition per Serving:

331 calories, 23 g fat, 5 g carbs, 2 g fiber, 26 g protein

Ingredients:

- ❖ fat free cream cheese (1 cup, softened)
- ❖ fat free mayonnaise (1 tbs)
- ❖ cooked chicken (2 cups, cubed)
- ❖ tomatoes (1 cup, seeded, sliced)
- ❖ Quinoa (1 (14 oz) can, cooked)
- ❖ romaine lettuce leaves (4)
- ❖ alfalfa sprouts (2 cups, rinsed, drained)
- ❖ whole wheat pita bread (4 round)

Directions:

1. In a bowl, combine mayonnaise and cream cheese until it is fully mixed.
2. Add chicken, tomatoes, Quinoa; mix well.
3. Slice the pita bread to form a pocket.
4. Fill your pitas with lettuce and chicken.
5. Top with alfalfa sprouts.
6. Serve.

Chicken and Asparagus Pasta

Yields: 4   Prep: 10 mins.   Cook: 22 mins.
Nutrition per Serving:
168 calories, 10 g fat, 7g carbs, 3 g fiber, 13 g protein

Ingredients:

- whole wheat penne pasta (1 lb.)
- olive oil (2 tbs)
- chicken breast halves (3/4 lb, sliced into strips)
- poultry seasoning (1/2 tsp)
- cloves garlic (4, minced)
- asparagus (1 1/2 cup, frozen, cut into 1 inch)
- peas (1 cup, frozen, thawed)
- parmesan cheese (1/4 cup, grated)

Directions:

1. Bring a pot of salted water to boil. Add pasta and cook to an al dente consistency according to package directions.
2. Heat one tablespoon olive oil in a non-stick pan over medium heat and cook chicken with poultry seasoning until golden.
3. Remove cooked chicken from the pan.
4. Add the remaining tablespoon of olive oil, garlic, asparagus and peas. Cook until vegetables are tender.
5. Put the chicken back into the pan with the asparagus mixture and cook for 2 minutes.
6. Put the pasta in a shallow pasta bowl and toss with chicken mixture. Top with parmesan cheese.

Turkey Florentine

Yields: 4   Prep: 15 mins.   Cook: 18 mins.

Nutrition per Serving:
593 calories, 8 g fat, 11 g carbs, 4 g fiber, 12 g protein

Ingredients:

- olive oil (2 tbs)
- zucchinis (2 medium, seeded, thinly sliced)
- green onions (1/2 cups, sliced)
- turkey breast (2 cups, cubed)
- salt (1/2 tsp)
- thyme (1/2 tsp, ground)
- pimento (2 tbs, chopped)
- cooked long-grain rice (3 cups)
- fresh baby spinach (4 cups)
- low fat parmesan cheese (1/4 cup, freshly grated)

Directions:

1. In a non-stick pan, heat olive oil over moderate heat. Add zucchini, turkey, and onions, stir ever now and then for 5 to 10 minutes.

2. Add salt, thyme, pimento, rice and spinach. Cook and stir for another 6 - 8 minutes or until heated through and spinach wilts.

3. Remove from heat, transfer to large serving bowl, and stir in cheese. Serve.

Chicken Lettuce Wraps

Yields: 2   Prep: 15 mins.   Cook: 0 mins.
Nutrition per Serving:
338 calories, 10 g fat, 39g carbs, 9 g fiber, 26 g protein

Ingredients:
- Mayonnaise (1/4 cup, low fat)
- lemon juice (2 tsp)
- white beans (1/2 cup, canned, cooked, drained)
- feta cheese (1/3 cup, crumbled)
- pimentos (2 tbs, chopped)
- lettuce leaves (8 large, washed, and dried)
- chicken breast strips (1/2 lb cooked, preferably grilled)

Directions:
1. In a medium bowl, combine mayonnaise and lemon juice.
2. Stir in beans, mashing slightly with fork.
3. Add cheese and pimentos and mix lightly.
4. Spread lettuce leaves evenly with bean mixture.
5. Top with chicken; roll up.
6. Serve.

Couscous with Turkey

Yields: 4   Prep: 20 mins.   Cook: 26 mins.

Nutrition per Serving:

469 calories, 24 g fat, 40 g carbs, 4 g fiber, 18 g protein

Ingredients:

- extra-virgin olive oil (4 tbs)
- turkey thighs (1 lb boneless, skinless, chopped)
- onion (1, chopped)
- cloves garlic (3, minced)
- carrots (1 cup, shredded)
- smoked paprika (1 tsp)
- ground cinnamon (1/8 tsp)
- salt (1/2 tsp)
- dried fruits (1 cup chopped, pitted dates, apricots)
- turkey stock (4 cups, divided)
- butter (2 tablespoons)
- couscous (1 1/2 cups)
- Italian parsley (1/2 cup, chopped)

Directions:

1. Set your oil to get hot on medium heat. Cook turkey and brown 3 to 4 minutes on each side.
2. Add onions, garlic, carrots, and season with spices and salt. Cook 6-8 minutes.
3. Stir the fruits into the turkey and vegetables, and 2 ½ cups of stock.
4. Allow to boil. Turn down the heat to low, cover and let it simmer for 10 minutes.
5. In a separate small saucepan, over medium heat, pour 1 ½ cups of stock and bring up to a boil then stir in the couscous.
6. Take the content off the heat and let it stand 5 minutes while the cover is on. Fluff with fork and serve with turkey.

Easy Turkey Chili

Yields: 4-6   Prep: 25 mins.   Cook: 47 mins.

Nutrition per Serving:

193 calories, 13 g fat, 5 g carbs, 1 g fiber, 16 g protein

Ingredients:

- olive oil (3 tbs)
- garlic cloves (4, minced)
- onion (1 medium, chopped)
- ground turkey (1 lb.)
- bay leaf (1)
- ground cumin (1 tsp)
- dried oregano (1 tsp)
- tomato (1, seeded and chopped)
- tomato sauce (1 (14 oz.) can)
- Pork broth (1 cup
- salt (1 tsp)
- red beans (2 (14 oz.) cans, drained and rinsed)

Directions:

1. Heat the oil over medium heat, in a large pot and cook the onions and garlic for 5 minutes.

2. Turn the heat from medium to high. Add oregano, bay leaf, turkey and cumin. Cook for 5-7 minutes or until turkey has browned.

3. Add broth, tomato sauce, tomato and salt. Once the pot is boiling, lower the heat to simmer. Let it simmer for about 20 minutes, covered.

4. If needed, add more water and beans and continue to simmer for 15 more minutes. Serve.

Ham, Bean and Cabbage Stew

Yields: 4   Prep: 15 mins.   Cook: 17 mins.
Nutrition per Serving:
543 calories, 21 g fat, 47g carbs, 8 g fiber, 40 g protein

Ingredients:

- extra virgin olive oil (1 tbs)
- smoked ham (8 oz, chopped)
- onion (1 large, chopped)
- stalks celery (2, sliced)
- cloves garlic (5, chopped finely)
- chicken broth (4 cups)
- tomatoes (1 (28 oz) can, seedless, drained)
- whole wheat pasta (3 cups)
- coleslaw (8 oz)
- kidney beans (2 (14 oz) cans)
- dried basil (1 tsp)
- dried rosemary (1 tsp)

Directions:

1. In a good size pot, heat olive oil over medium heat. Cook ham, onion, celery and garlic stirring occasionally, until vegetables are tender.

2. Stir in broth and tomatoes, breaking up tomatoes. Stir the pasta in, heat to boiling and turn down the heat low.

3. Cover and simmer about 10 minutes or until pasta is tender. Stir in coleslaw, beans, basil and oregano.

4. Bring stew to a boil and reduce heat to low. Simmer uncovered about 5-7 minutes or until cabbage is tender.

Grilled Fish Tacos

Yields: 4   Prep: 25 mins.   Cook: 6 mins.
Nutrition per Serving:
356 calories, 9 g fat, 57g carbs, 17 g fiber, 15 g protein

Ingredients:
- Salt (1/4 tsp)
- Juice of 1/2 lemon
- olive oil (2 tbs)
- trout filets (4, rinsed and dried)
- red onion (1/2 cup, chopped)
- jicama (1/2 cup, peeled, chopped)
- red bell pepper (1/3 cup, chopped)
- fresh cilantro (2/3 cup, finely chopped)
- black beans (1 cup, drained and rinsed)
- Zest and juice (1/2 lime)
- plain yogurt (1 tbs, non-fat)
- whole wheat tortillas (8, warmed)

Directions:
1. Combine your oil, lemon juice and salt.
2. Then pour all of that over the fish fillets and let it marinate for a few minutes.
3. Cook the fish on both side for 3 minutes. In another bowl, combine onion, bell pepper, jicama, cilantro, yogurt and zest and juice of lime to make a salsa.
4. Add your fish on top of a warm tortilla. Top with salsa and fold in half before serving.

Pasta with Turkey and Olives

Yields: 4   Prep: 20 mins.   Cook: 30 mins.
Nutrition per Serving:
165 calories, 4 g fat, 18 g carbs, 3 g fiber, 14 g protein

Ingredients:

- whole wheat pasta (1 lb, uncooked)
- olive oil (2 tsp)
- onion (1 large, peeled, chopped finely)
- cloves garlic (4, peeled, finely chopped)
- turkey breast (1 lb, cut into chunks)
- basil (1 tsp, dried)

- rosemary (1 tsp, dried)
- black olives (12 med, pitted)
- green bell pepper (1 med, seeded and chopped)
- tomatoes (1 (14 oz) can, seedless, chopped)
- chicken broth (1 can)
- Romano cheese (1/2 cup, shredded)

Directions:

1. Bring a salted water to boil in a large pot. Add pasta and cook until al dente follow instruction according to the package.
2. While pasta cooks, heat the oil in a large pan over medium heat. Add the garlic and onion. Cook for 6 minutes.
3. Add the turkey, rosemary and basil. Cook for about 8 minutes.
4. Stir in the olives, tomatoes and green pepper and cook for 2 minutes. In the pan add the chicken broth, heat the pan to a boil.
5. Reduce half of the liquid by boiling for 7 minutes. When pasta is done, add to sauce mixture.
6. Toss until pasta is evenly mixed with sauce. Top with cheese and serve.

Pasta with Escarole, Beans and Turkey

Yields: 4   Prep: 20 mins.   Cook: 16mins.

Nutrition per Serving:
289 calories, 6 g fat,36 g carbs, 16 g fiber, 24 g protein

Ingredients:
- ❖ whole-wheat bowtie pasta (3/4 pound)
- ❖ olive oil (1 tbs)
- ❖ onion (1/2 medium, chopped)
- ❖ cloves garlic (3, minced)
- ❖ turkey (6 oz, ground)
- ❖ head escarole (1 medium, rinsed, drained and chopped)
- ❖ cannellini beans (1(14oz) can, drained and rinsed)
- ❖ chicken broth (1 1/2 cups)
- ❖ rosemary (1 tbs, chopped)
- ❖ salt (1/2 tsp)
- ❖ Parmesan cheese (1/4 cup, grated)

Directions:
1. Bring a salted water to boil in a pot. Add the pasta and follow the cooking instruction on the package.
2. Drain. In a large non-stick pan, heat olive oil over medium heat.
3. Add onion and cook until softened, add garlic and turkey and cook until it browns, about 5 minutes.
4. Add the escarole and cook it for 4 minutes. Add the beans, 1 cup of turkey stock, rosemary, and salt.
5. Simmer until the mixture is slightly thickened. Add the pasta and toss well, thin the sauce with the additional 1/2 cup stock if needed.
6. Top with parmesan cheese. Serve.

Rice Bowl with Shrimp and Peas

Yields: 4   Prep: 15 mins.   Cook: 48 mins.
Nutrition per Serving:
143 calories, 4 g fat, 19g carbs, 2 g fiber, 7 g protein

Ingredients:

- long-grain brown rice (1 cup)
- soy sauce (1/4 cup)
- fresh lemon juice (1/4 cup)
- rice vinegar (2 tbs)
- honey (2 tbs)
- olive oil (1 tbs)
- shrimp (1 lb, medium, cleaned, peeled, deveined)
- snow peas (8 oz, thawed if frozen, cut in halves)
- piece fresh ginger (1 (1-inch long) shredded)
- Hass avocado (1, chopped)

Directions:

1. Boil 2 cups of water in a saucepan. Add the rice and cover and turn the heat down to simmer.
2. Cook the rice for about 35-45 minutes. In a bowl, fully combine soy sauce, lemon juice, honey, and vinegar.
3. Set your olive oil to get hot on medium heat in a non-stick pan.
4. Add in your shrimp, ginger and peas then cook for about 3 minutes (or until shrimp becomes pink).
5. Transfer rice to serving bowls, then top with avocado and shrimp mixture. Serve the sauce on the side.

Roasted Chicken and Vegetables

Yields: 4   Prep: 15 mins.   Cook: 55 mins.

Nutrition per Serving:

147 calories, 11 g fat, 13g carbs, 3 g fiber, 2 g protein

Ingredients:

- Roma tomatoes (6, seedless, quartered)
- Zucchini (3 medium, chopped coarsely)
- Potatoes (2 large, unpeeled, quartered)
- olive oil (3 tbs, divided)
- salt (3/4 tsp, divided)
- cloves garlic (4, finely minced)
- fresh rosemary (1 tbs, chopped)
- fresh thyme (1 tbs, leaves taken off sprig)
- lemon zest (1 tsp)
- lemon juice (1 tbs)
- chicken breast halves (4, skinless)

Directions:

1. Preheat oven to 375F degrees. Put tomatoes, zucchini and potatoes in a roasting pan, and toss with 2 tbs of oil and 1/4 tsp salt.
2. Combine lemon zest, thyme, rosemary, garlic, oil, salt and lemon juice. Pour this mixture over chicken.
3. Place chicken in pan with vegetables. Bake in oven for 30 minutes.
4. Stir chicken and vegetables and bake another 25 minutes, or until chicken is cooked through and vegetables are tender.

Shrimp and Black Bean Nachos

Yields: 4   Prep: 25 mins.   Cook: 0 mins.

Nutrition per Serving:

172 calories, 14 g fat, 12 g carbs, 5 g fiber, 4 g protein

Ingredients:

- ❖ Cilantro (3/4 cup, fresh chopped)
- ❖ red onion (1/2 cup, diced)
- ❖ lime juice (2 tbs)
- ❖ olive oil (1 tbs)
- ❖ Worcestershire sauce (1 tsp)
- ❖ salt (1/2 tsp)
- ❖ shrimp (3/4 lb medium, peeled, cooked, and chopped)
- ❖ tomatoes (2 cups, seeded, diced)
- ❖ avocado (1/2 cup, diced)
- ❖ black bean (1 (15 oz) can, rinsed and drained)
- ❖ ground cumin (1/2 tsp)
- ❖ baked tortilla chips (4 cup)

Directions:

1. In a bowl combine cilantro, onion, lime juice, oil, Worcestershire sauce, shrimp and salt. Cover and refrigerate for 30 minutes.

2. Add tomato and avocado; stir well. Place the cumin and beans in a food processor, and process until smooth.

3. Spread 1-teaspoon black-bean mixture on each chip. Top with 1-tablespoon shrimp mixture. Serve.

Southwestern Chicken Pitas

Yields: 6   Prep: 15 mins.   Cook: 0 mins.

Nutrition per Serving:

345 calories, 12 g fat, 22 g carbs, 5 g fiber, 35 g protein

Ingredients:

- ❖ black beans (1 (15 oz) can, drained, rinsed)
- ❖ red bell pepper (1/2 cup, chopped, seeded)
- ❖ fresh lime juice (3 tbs)
- ❖ fresh cilantro leaves (2 tbs, minced)
- ❖ canola oil (2 tbs)
- ❖ chicken breasts (4, boneless, halved, skinless)
- ❖ round whole wheat pita bread (4)
- ❖ low-fat provolone cheese (6 slices, cut in halves)

Directions:

1. In a bowl, combine beans, bell pepper, lime juice, and cilantro. Set aside. In a pan, heat up the oil over medium heat.
2. Cook chicken in pan until golden brown. Set aside for 10 without cutting. Warm pita bread in oven.
3. Cut chicken into slices. Place half a slice of cheese in center of one pita bread.
4. Top off the sandwich with bean mixture the chicken breast slices. Roll up tightly. Cut in half and serve.

Spaghetti with Zucchini

Yields: 4   Prep: 10 mins.   Cook: 12 mins.
Nutrition per Serving:
156 calories, 11 g fat, 11 g carbs, 2 g fiber, 5 g protein

Ingredients:

- whole wheat spaghetti (1 lb)
- zucchini (2 medium, grated, water, squeezed out)
- butter (2 tbs)
- olive oil (1 tbs)
- cloves garlic (2, minced)
- Parmesan cheese (1/2 cup, freshly grated)

Directions:

1. Bring a salted water to boil in a pot. Add pasta and cook until it is al dente or follow the instructions on the package.
2. While pasta cooks, in a large non-stick pan, heat the oil and butter together. Add in the zucchini and allow cook for 3 minutes.
3. Add in your garlic and continue to cook for another minute, stirring constantly. Add in a half of your parmesan cheese.
4. Transfer past to a serving bowl. Add your zucchini mixture. Toss then garnish with remaining parmesan cheese. Enjoy!

Summer Spaghetti

Yields: 4   Prep: 15 mins.   Cook: 8 mins.

Nutrition per Serving:
548 calories, 57 g fat, 14 g carbs, 3 g fiber, 3 g protein

Ingredients:

- whole wheat spaghetti (1 lb)
- olive oil (1/4 cup)
- shallot (1, minced)
- cloves garlic (2, minced)
- zucchini (1 medium, chopped)
- summer squash (1 medium, chopped)
- green beans (1/2 lb, ends cut)
- basil (1/4 cup, coarsely chopped)
- salt (1/2 tsp)
- lemon (1/2 medium, juiced)
- unsalted butter (2 tbs, room temperature)
- freshly grated lemon peel

Directions:

1. Bring a salted water to boil in a pot. Add pasta and cook until it is al dente or follow the instructions on the package.

2. Heat up the oil over medium heat in a large pan. Add in your garlic and shallot, then stir frequently until fragrant (about 2 minutes).

3. Add the zucchini, squash, green beans, and basil. Continue to cook, stir occasionally, until all vegetables are tender.

4. Season vegetables with salt and lemon juice. In a large shallow pasta bowl, immediately place the sautéed vegetables with all their juices.

5. Add the butter and linguine, toss to mix well and serve immediately.

White Bean Tortellini

Yields: 4   Prep: 20 mins.   Cook: 1 hr. 33 mins.

Nutrition per Serving:

489 calories, 10 g fat, 68 g carbs, 17 g fiber, 33 g protein

Ingredients:

- olive oil (2 tbs)
- white beans (2 cups, uncooked)
- onion (1 small, chopped)
- garlic cloves (2, finely chopped)
- tomatoes (1 cup, seeded and chopped)
- tomato paste (2 tbs)
- chicken broth (7 cups)
- bay leaf (1)
- tortellini (1 lb, with the filling of your choice)
- fresh basil (¼ cup, chopped)

Directions:

1. Soak the beans in water for 8 hours. Drain the beans once you are ready to us it. Heat up the olive oil over medium heat.
2. Add the onion and let it cook for 3 minutes. Mix in the garlic and cook for another minute.
3. Add the tomatoes and tomato paste, stir and cook for a few minutes.
4. Add beans, chicken broth, and bay leaf then allow to boil. Once boiling, lower heat then allow to simmer, without the cover, for another hour and a half.
5. Transfer your mixture to your blender and process into a puree.
6. Adjust the consistency with more stock if necessary.
7. Set a large pot on with salted water and allow to boil. Add in your tortellini and cook as directed by the package.
8. Serve by topping with sauce and basil. Enjoy.

Pink Salmon Cakes & Potatoes

Yields: 4   Prep: 20 mins.   Cook: 16 mins.
Nutrition per Serving:
432 calories, 34 g fat, 29 g carbs, 2 g fiber, 6 g protein

Ingredients:
For Pink salmon Cakes:
- ❖ canola oil (3 tbs)
- ❖ pink salmon fish (2 (6 oz) cans, drained)
- ❖ egg (1, beaten)
- ❖ green onions (2 tablespoons, diced)
- ❖ mayonnaise (1/4 cup, non-fat)
- ❖ whole wheat bread (1/2 cup, cut into small pieces)

- ❖ Lemon juice, optional
For Smashed Potatoes:
- ❖ Potatoes (2 large, unpeeled, chopped)
- ❖ salt (2 tsp)
- ❖ low fat milk (1/2 cup)
- ❖ unsalted butter (3 tablespoons)

Directions:
1. Cook potatoes in a small saucepan until tender. Drain.
2. Place potatoes back in pan. Heat the butter and milk in microwave until hot.
3. Roughly smash the potatoes with a potato smasher while adding hot liquid until combined and set aside.
4. Combine egg, pink salmon, lemon juice, green onions, mayonnaise, breadcrumbs, and egg in a bowl.
5. Form into patties. Allow to refrigerate and become firm for 10 minutes.
6. Heat oil over medium heat, cook patties until golden brown, about 2 minutes on each side. Serve with potatoes.

Turkey and Barley Casserole

Yields: 4   Prep: 15 mins.   Cook: 1 hr. 10 mins.

Nutrition per Serving:

361 calories, 11 g fat, 42 g carbs, 10 g fiber, 30 g protein

Ingredients:

- ground turkey (3/4 lb)
- salt (1/2 tsp)
- onion (1, chopped finely)
- carrots (2, chopped)
- stalks celery (2, chopped)
- green bell pepper (1, seeded and chopped)
- button mushrooms (12, quartered)
- chicken stock (2 1/2 cups)
- barley (1 cup)
- poultry seasoning (1 tsp)
- bay leaf (1)

Directions:

1. Preheat oven to 375F degrees. Over medium heat, cook ground turkey with salt until browned, about 5 minutes, in a pan.
2. Add green peppers, celery, carrots and onions. Cook until tender, about 5 minutes.
3. Add bay leaf, poultry seasoning, barley, stock and mushrooms.
4. Mix together and place the mixture in a baking dish. Cover and bake in the preheated oven for 1 hour. Serve.

Lemon Chicken

Yields: 4   Prep: 10 mins.   Cook: 10 mins.
Nutrition per Serving:
184 calories, 9 g fat, 15 g carbs, 2 g fiber, 9 g protein

Ingredients:

- whole wheat pasta (1 lb)
- olive oil (2 tsp)
- onion (1 medium, chopped)
- Dijon mustard (1 tbs)
- whole wheat flour (2 tbs)
- chicken broth (2 cups)
- lemon juice (1/4 cup)

- peas (12 oz, frozen and thawed)
- Italian parsley (1/4 cup fresh, chopped)
- chicken (12 oz cooked, chopped)

Directions:

1. Bring a salted water to boil in a pot. Add and cook the pasta according to the package.
2. Set your olive oil in a non-stick pan to get hot on medium heat. Stir in the onion and cook for 3 minutes.
3. Stir in your flour and Dijon mustard. Slowly add in your chicken broth while whisking to avoid clumps.
4. Bring the broth to a boil and stir in the lemon juice, parsley, and peas. Add the cooked pasta and chicken to the sauce and serve.

Almond Salad

Yields: 1   Prep: 10 mins.   Cook: 0 mins.
Nutrition per Serving:
101 calories, 6 g fat, 10g carbs, 3 g fiber, 2 g protein

Ingredients:
- Blanched almonds (1½ cups, chopped)
- Olives (18)
- Celery (1½ cups, cut fine)
- Salad dressing (1 tbs)
- Lettuce

Directions:
1. Stone and chop the olives. Add the almonds and the celery. Mix with salad dressing and serve on the lettuce.

Vegetarian Nuttolene Salad

Yields: 1   Prep: 10 mins.   Cook: 0 mins.
Nutrition per Serving:
55 calories, 0 g fat, 12 g carbs, 3 g fiber, 2 g protein

Ingredients:
- Nuttolene (¼ pound, Chopped)
- Celery (⅔ cup, Chopped)
- Protose (½ pound, Chopped)
- Onion (1 small teaspoonful, Grated)
- Lemons juice (2)
- Salt.
- Mayonnaise (2 tablespoonfuls)

Directions:
1. Mix all the ingredients together, then add the mayonnaise dressing last. Serve

Nutty Green Salad

Yields: 4 Prep: 5 mins. Cook: 0 mins.
Nutrition per Serving:
252 calories, 2 g fat, 11 g carbs, 4 g fiber, 10 g protein

Ingredients:
- ❖ Walnut meats (1 cup)
- ❖ French peas (1 can)
- ❖ Mayonnaise (1 tbs)
- ❖ Lettuce (1 medium)

Directions:
1. Put the walnut meats in extreme hot water for fifteen minutes.
2. Remove the skins, then cut it into pieces. Set your peas to scald then set aside.
3. Drain the water from the peas, and let it get cold; then mix with the walnuts.
4. Add the mayonnaise dressing and mix thoroughly. Serve on lettuce.

Asian Chicken Salad

Yields: 1 Prep: 15 mins. Cook: 0 mins.
Nutrition per Serving:
384 calories, 4 g fat, 68g carbs, 10 g fiber, 25 g protein

Ingredients:
- ❖ romaine lettuce (1 cup, chopped)
- ❖ carrot (1, shredded)
- ❖ celery (1, sliced thinly)
- ❖ red pepper (1/4 cup, seeded, sliced thinly)
- ❖ chicken breast (1/2 cup, cooked, cut into strips)
- ❖ mangos (1/4 cup, chopped)
- ❖ lime and ginger dressing (2 tbsp)

Directions:
1. Toss together all ingredients in a medium bowl until combined. Serve alone or with whole wheat bread slices.

Bean and Couscous Salad

Yields: 4   Prep: 15 mins.   Cook: 0 mins.
Nutrition per Serving:
637 calories, 15 g fat, 101 g carbs, 18 g fiber, 28 g protein

Ingredients:

- couscous (1 cup)
- boiling water (1 1/2 cups)
- sweet yellow peppers (1 cup, seeded and chopped)
- black beans (2 cups, cooked)
- onion (1 small, chopped)
- tomatoes (2 cups, seeded and chopped)
- garlic cloves (2 medium, minced)
- rice vinegar (1/2 cup)
- olive oil (1/4 cup)
- salt (1/2 tsp)

Directions:

1. In a large bowl, place the couscous with boiling water. Cover and wait until couscous have absorbed all the water.
2. Place couscous in a bowl and add the remaining ingredients. Mix well. Serve.

Strawberry & Apple Salad

Yields: 2   Prep: 10 mins.   Cook: 0 mins.
Nutrition per Serving:
184 calories, 11 g fat, 23 g carbs, 4 g fiber, 4 g protein

Ingredients:

- Ripe strawberries (1½ cups)
- Fresh apple (cut in small cubes, 1½ cups)
- Brazil nuts (12, blanched and thinly sliced)
- Lemon juice (4 tablespoonfuls)
- Lettuce
- Dressing, (1 tablespoonful)

Directions:

1. Cut the apples and strawberries and add Brazil nuts that have been marinated in lemon juice.
2. Shape your lettuce into a rose, and fill the lettuce with the mixture above, and cover with a spoonful salad dressing.

Cucumber Peach Salad

Yields: 4   Prep: 30 mins.   Cook: 0 mins.

Nutrition per Serving:

182 calories, 11 g fat, 23g carbs, 3 g fiber, 6 g protein

Ingredients:

- ❖ Avocados (2 large, pitted and diced)
- ❖ Peach (1, unpeeled, pitted and diced)
- ❖ Gala pear (1, unpeeled, cored and diced)
- ❖ Cantaloupe (1 cup, chopped)
- ❖ Shallot (1, chopped finely)
- ❖ English cucumber (1, chopped)
- ❖ fresh lime juice (1/4 cup)
- ❖ fresh mint (1/4 cup, chopped)
- ❖ Large lettuce leaves

Directions:

1. In a medium bowl, combine all ingredients except the lettuce leaves. Sprinkle the mint and lime juice.
2. Toss until combine. Let salad sit at least 10-20 minutes. Serve over 2 leaves of lettuce per serving.

String bean Potato Salad

Yields: 4-6   Prep: 15 mins.   Cook: 7 mins.
Nutrition per Serving:
142 calories, 11 g fat, 10g carbs, 1 g fiber, 1 g protein

Ingredients:

- string beans (1 1/2 lbs, slender)
- red potatoes (6 small, unpeeled, cubed)
- red onion (1 small, thinly sliced lengthwise)
- extra virgin olive oil (1/3 cup)
- red wine vinegar (1/4 cup)
- rice vinegar (1/4 cup)
- garlic salt (1 tbs)
- sugar (1 tsp)

Directions:

1. In a pot of boiling water, cook potatoes and string beans about 7 minutes.
2. Drain the contents and run cold water on the beans only to stop cooking process. Drain and set it aside.
3. In a large salad bowl, combine beans, potatoes and onions. For dressing, in a bowl, whisk together olive oil, vinegars, garlic salt and sugar.
4. Toss the vegetables and dressing together until coated. Refrigerate one hour prior to serving.

Bean and Tomato Salad

Yields: 4   Prep: 10 mins.   Cook: 0 mins.
Nutrition per Serving:
201 calories, 14 g fat, 18 g carbs, 4 g fiber, 4 g protein

Ingredients:

- Tomatoes (4 medium, seeded and chopped)
- garbanzos (2 (14 oz) cans, drained and rinsed)
- red onions (1/4 cup, chopped finely)
- Italian parsley (1 cup, chopped finely)
- lemon Juice (2 tbs)
- extra virgin olive oil (1/4 cup)
- salt (1/2 tsp)

Directions:

1. Combine your parsley, onions, beans and tomato. Set aside. In another bowl whisk together salt, olive oil and lemon juice.
2. Pour dressing over vegetables. Mix and serve.

Ricotta & Cannellini Salad

Yields: 6   Prep: 15 mins.   Cook: 0 mins.
Nutrition per Serving:
160 calories, 11 g fat, 10 g carbs, 2 g fiber, 6 g protein

Ingredients:

- plain yogurt (2 tbs, low fat)
- extra virgin olive oil (3 tbs)
- fresh lemon juice (2 tbs)
- oregano (3/4 tsp, ground)
- fresh mint (1 tbs, shredded)
- white cannellini beans (2 (14 oz) cans, drained and rinsed)
- red onions (1/2 cup, thinly sliced)
- tomatoes (3 medium, seeded and chopped)
- Greek olives (1/4 cup, pitted)
- ricotta cheese (1/2 cup, crumbled)
- spinach leaves (2 cups)

Directions:

1. In large bowl, combine yogurt, olive oil, lemon juice, oregano, and mint; whisk well.
2. Add onion, beans, tomato, ricotta cheese and olives; toss lightly.
3. Refrigerate for at least one hour. Serve on a bed of spinach.

Bean & Crayfish Salad

Yields: 6   Prep: 15 mins.   Cook: 5 mins.
Nutrition per Serving:
334 calories, 34 g fat, 7 g carbs, 3 g fiber, 3 g protein

Ingredients:

- Crayfish (1 1/2 lbs, large, cleaned, de-veined and peeled)
- olive oil (1/2 cup)
- garlic (2 cloves, minced)
- salt (1/2 tsp)
- shallots (2, minced)
- fresh Italian parsley (1 tbs, chopped)
- fresh sage leaves (1 1/2 tbs, chopped)
- red wine vinegar (1 tbs)
- cannellini beans (2 (14 oz) cans, drained and rinsed)

Directions:

1. In a glass dish, combine 1/4 teaspoon of salt, garlic and 1/4 cup of the olive oil. Add the crayfish and mix well. Set aside.
2. In a medium bowl, combine the shallots with the remaining 1/4 cup oil and 1/4 teaspoon salt, parsley, sage, and vinegar.
3. Gently stir in the beans. Grill the crayfish over medium heat, turning once, about 3-5 minutes.
4. Serve the crayfish with the bean salad.

Tropical Black Bean Salad

Yields: 6   Prep: 15 mins.   Cook: 0 mins.
Nutrition per Serving:
526 calories, 7 g fat, 91 g carbs, 21 g fiber, 29 g protein

Ingredients:
- black beans (2 (14 oz) cans, drained and rinsed)
- mangoes (4 medium, peeled and diced)
- fresh Italian parsley (1 cup, minced)
- scallions (2 small, chopped finely)
- red peppers (2 medium, seeded and diced)
- extra virgin olive oil (2 tbs)
- balsamic vinegar (1/2 cup)
- salt (1/4 tsp)

Directions:
1. In a large salad bowl, combine beans with mangoes, parsley, scallions, and red bell peppers.
2. In a separate small bowl, whisk together the oil, vinegar and salt. Pour over vegetables and mix well. Serve.

Creamy Green Salad

Yields: 1   Prep: 10 mins.   Cook: 0 mins.
Nutrition per Serving:
270 calories, 12 g fat, 40 g carbs, 9 g fiber, 4 g protein

Ingredients:
- Pears (1½ cups, cut in dice)
- Lemon juice (½ cup)
- Lettuce
- Celery (1½ cups, cut in dice)
- Mayonnaise dressing (1 tbs.)

Directions:
1. Mix the lemon juice, celery, and pears together. Pour the mayonnaise dressing. Serve on the lettuce.

Green Goodness Salad

Yields: 2   Prep: 10 mins.   Cook: 0 mins.

Nutrition per Serving:
211 calories, 14 g fat, 21 g carbs, 10 g fiber, 7 g protein

Ingredients:
- ❖ Spinach (1 cup, chopped)
- ❖ Kale (1 cup, chopped)
- ❖ Avocado (1 medium, diced)
- ❖ Cucumber (1 medium, sliced)
- ❖ Onion (1 medium, diced)
- ❖ Broccoli (1 cup, florets)

Directions:
1. In a large bowl, mix desired amount of spinach, avocado, cucumber, onion, and broccoli.
2. Top with lemon and olive oil as dressing

Conclusion

Congratulations on making it all the way to the end of the Diverticulitis Cookbook: Proven and Delicious Diverticulitis Diet Recipes to Prevent Flare-Ups and Improve Gut Health. 3-Phase Diet Guide with Easy to Find Ingredients and a 21-Day Action Plan.

I hope that you were able to find vale in the information provided and that you were able to utilize the recipes featured to get you further along in your Diverticulitis journey.

If you enjoyed the Diverticulitis Cookbook, please take a moment to share your thoughts on Amazon by leaving a review.

Thank you and have a great day.